SILENT REVOLUTION

SILENT REVOLUTION

The Transformation of
DIVORCE LAW
in the United States

HERBERT JACOB

THE UNIVERSITY OF CHICAGO PRESS
CHICAGO AND LONDON

HERBERT JACOB is professor of political science at
Northwestern University. He is the author or editor of
over a dozen monographs and textbooks, including
Felony Justice (with James Eisenstein) and *The
Frustration of Policy: Responses to Crime by American
Cities.*

The University of Chicago Press, Chicago 60637
The University of Chicago Press, Ltd., London

97 96 95 94 93 92 91 90 89 88   5 4 3 2 1

Library of Congress Cataloging-in-Publication Data
Jacob, Herbert. 1933–
    Silent revolution: the transformation of divorce law in the
United States / Herbert Jacob.
        p. cm.
    Includes index.
    ISBN 0-226-38951-0
    1. Divorce—Law and legislation—United States. I. Title
KF535.J33   1988
346.7301'66—dc19
[347.306166]   87-37483
                                                           CIP

For J.B., D.S., J.E., and M.M.

Contents

Acknowledgments

Work on this book began when I was invited to spend three months at the Centre for Socio-Legal Studies at Oxford University in 1981. It continued under two grants from the National Science Foundation (nos. SES–83–19321 and SES–85–16112) and also was supported by the funds of the Glenn B. and Cleone Orr Hawkins Chair of Political Science at the University of Wisconsin, Madison, as well as by research support from Northwestern University. I have also benefited greatly from the supportive environment provided by the Center for Urban Affairs and Policy Research at Northwestern University. All of these patrons are responsible for the fruits of my labor but none is answerable for my opinions and interpretations.

The story this book tells would not have been unraveled without the generous cooperation of the many participants in divorce law reform who allowed me to interview them and to inspect their papers. In addition, several important libraries and archives made their materials available to me. To all those who are listed in the Appendix, as well as to the many staff members who are not, I wish to express my gratitude.

After I had chosen the title, I discovered that my good friend Lawrence Friedman had used the same words to describe the passage of the Married Women's Property Acts in the nineteenth century in his *History of American Law.* My thanks to him for his subliminal suggestion.

In the course of this work, I have been assisted by Hugh Bohlender, Georgia Duerst-Lahti, Jo Perry, Susan Peterson,

Ron Wohl, and Laura Wolliver. They performed the many tiresome tasks such a research project entails with good cheer and great care.

Many colleagues read all or parts of this manuscript. I learned and profited from all of them. My wife was especially helpful because of her insights into the world of divorce, gained through years of professional involvement in the divorce process as a mediator and counselor. To all go my thanks for their assistance and my apologies for any errors that remain.

1

Introduction: The Silent Revolution

Self-appointed prophets preaching the doom of the family appear in every generation. They provide text for ministers' sermons and topics for women's supplements of daily newspapers. Yet few policy makers pay attention because conventional familial patterns appeared to survive despite the forecasts of disaster.

Not so now. Census reports as well as doomsayers are noting substantial changes in American life-styles.[1] But less noticed by social commentators, editors, or talk-show hosts, have been the radical changes in legal expectations about family life. The new norms bear scant resemblance to the old.

Consider, for instance, the consequences when a husband or wife is caught committing adultery. In all states the adulterer has just as much standing to sue for divorce as the "innocent" party, and evidence about such misbehavior may not even be introduced in the divorce hearings in fourteen states. Even if the innocent party objects, no barrier exists to their getting a divorce. In most states, no penalty is attached to adulterous behavior when the couple's property is divided, when decisions are made about alimony, or when the court determines who should have custody of the children. Adultery and other marital misbehavior is no longer punished by the law of divorce. Indeed, the concept of fault has been banished. Divorces are usually no longer issued on a basis of marital misbehavior; courts grant them simply when one or both spouses allege that their marriage has been irretrievably broken by irreconcilable differences.

Other changes are equally dramatic. For most of the last century, the law, courts, and ordinary citizens assumed that mothers were better suited to be guardians for their children when a family broke apart. Child care was woman's work which most men did not care to pursue and for which many had little aptitude. Today the law usually makes no such an assumption, which had been called the "tender years doctrine." The law now presumes mothers and fathers equally qualified to care for children of any age unless evidence to the contrary is presented. Moreover, the law in a growing number of states no longer considers sole custody of children by mother or father to be the norm. In an increasing number of cases, custody no longer is awarded exclusively to either mother or father; instead, both retain at least legal custody of their children.

Change has not only characterized the manner in which couples obtain divorces and the fate of their children. It has also breached conventional norms of the kernel of American life—property. Traditionally, all but the handful of community property states had a simple rule for determining who owned the couple's property when a marriage ended. The person who held title to the property owned it, although an innocent wife might be granted her dower's portion, usually less than one-third of her ex-husband's real property. Those relatively simple guidelines have been almost universally replaced by much more complex rules. A family's property is now regarded as "marital property" belonging to both husband and wife regardless of title. Marital property normally includes everything acquired during the marriage excepts gifts or inheritances. Marital property may be divided in an equitable or an equal manner, depending on the details of the law in a particular state. In establishing the concept of marital rather than individual property, the law has also abandoned the rule that allocates property according to monetary contributions toward its acquisition. In many states, statutes explicitly mandate that a homemaker's non-monetary contributions be counted the same as the wage earner's salary or income.

Even the well-established rule that wives are eligible for continued support from their husbands has been overturned.
Alimony laws no longer refer to gender, and if the husband is
dependent upon the wife, the wife may be ordered to pay him
alimony. Indeed, the term alimony itself has been replaced with
"spousal support" or "maintenance." Its permanence has also
been breached. It is no longer considered a lifelong commitment to be ended only upon remarriage of the recipient.
Rather, maintenance has become a transition payment
intended to help an ex-spouse become self-sufficient. It often
does not extend beyond three or five years, and during that
time it frequently is gradually diminished.

Most of these laws were enacted after 1965. No party platform or social protest spurred legislators to accept them.
Neither national politicians nor Congress played a part in their
adoption. No bureaucracy or national interest group promoted them. Little political conflict accompanied them. While
controversy raged about civil rights, Vietnam, Watergate, state
taxation, abortion, the Equal Rights Amendment, Iranian hos-
tages, and the withdrawal of government involvement from
the private sector by the Reagan administration, state legislators quietly adopted the radically new rules for divorce.

The distance between these new rules and their traditional
predecessors is immense and can only be appreciated by examining the conventional forerunners. One change they validated
was the wife's transition from subordinate to equal. That
change occurred gradually both in social fact and in the law. In
the early nineteenth century, wives were clearly subordinate to
their husbands.[2] Upon marriage, a woman lost her maiden
name and took up the identity of her husband.[3] Her name
change signified not only a new identity but also subordination
to her husband in many matters. For instance, both custom and
law required a wife to live wherever her husband chose. When
a husband moved to a new neighborhood or city, his wife and
children were obliged to move with him. Husbands had responsibility for supporting their families, but they did not have
to live up to specific standards; the living standard was the husband's choice. In return, wives were expected to maintain the
home and to submit to their husband's sexual demands. Final-

ly, wives originally had no control over property, even when they brought it with them into marriage. As late as 1945, a New Jersey court could write:

The plaintiff [husband] is the master of his household. He is the managing head, with control and power to preserve the family relation, to protect its members and to guide their conduct. He has the obligation and responsibility of supporting, maintaining and protecting the family and the correlative right to exclude intruders and unwanted visitors from the home despite the whims of the wife.[4]

Property rules were the first element of this legal patriarchy to change with the passage of Married Women's Property Acts in the last half of the nineteenth century.[5] Those laws gave wives control over property they brought into marriage and that they earned outside the home (although a husband retained authority to prohibit his wife from working outside the home). The Married Women's Property Acts, however, did not emancipate wives, for the law preserved the basic hierarchical structure of marital responsibilities and privileges which unmistakably placed husbands on top and wives below. That legal structure remained essentially unchanged until the mid-twentieth century.[6]

Another fundamental difference of nineteenth-century family law was its assumption that marriage was permanent. As we shall see in the next chapter, permanence involved a shorter period of time in the nineteenth century than in the twentieth. Most marriages ended because a spouse died rather than as a result of the desire by husband or wife to try some other living arrangement. Probate law, therefore, was more important than divorce law in determining the distribution of property. However, because of her subordinate status and the assumption that marriages were permanent, an abandoned wife who was innocent of marital offenses could claim continued maintenance from her former husband until another man took over the support obligation by marrying her, although that did not guarantee that most such women could collect their money.

Since marriage was considered permanent, it could only be dissolved with considerable difficulty. Husband or wife had to be guilty of serious misbehavior to justify a divorce. Adultery always qualified; over the course of the nineteenth century, other grounds for divorce were added to include many kinds of offending behavior, such as physical and mental abuse, drunkenness, imprisonment, drug addiction, desertion, or insanity.[7] These grounds, however, presumed that one spouse committed them while the other remained innocent. If both were proved guilty—as might happen when both sued for divorce and claimed the other had committed a marital offense—neither qualified for divorce. In addition, committing a marital offense had serious post-divorce consequences, especially for wives. Guilty wives were often penalized by denial of alimony and by getting little or none of the couple's property. Custody of children also could be denied to the sinful parent. Thus divorce was a very serious matter which impugned reputations and had the potential of depriving men and women of property and children.

The contrast with contemporary law could not be starker. Equality has replaced hierarchy as the guiding principle of family law. Spouses no longer need to point the finger of blame at one another. Blame is not considered in determining maintenance, property division, or custody of children. Divorce rarely stigmatizes and has become easy and often quick. Marriage is no longer presumed to be a lifelong commitment.

Both the old and the new laws reflect considerable ambiguity about the propriety of governmental intrusion into private affairs. Family life has always been among the most private spheres, while at the same time it has also been heavily regulated by government. The ambiguity dates from the inclusion of family life in the medieval church's reach. Marriage was (and is) a sacrament for many Christians; divorce as we know it was absolutely prohibited.[8] In medieval England, the common-law courts of the crown concentrated on matters involving land, while church courts retained jurisdiction over marriage and children. When government took over church interests in marriage and divorce, public law replaced church law. For the most part, however, public law simply echoed what had been church doctrine. Thus, in England divorce remained practically unavailable until the middle of the nineteenth century.[9] Much of the law surrounding the regulation of marriages also had religious roots, such as the laws prohibiting incestuous marriages. However, secular concerns were evident with the state's interest in ensuring the legitimation of children, which had important consequences for the inheritance of property and the ability to clear title so that property could be bought and sold with the confidence that no other claims to it would arise. Secular interests were also reflected in the regulation of the age of marriage without parental consent and in the requirement for health examinations.

Nevertheless, most but not all of family life remained out of the reach of the state's agents in England and the United States as long as the family members did not seriously transgress broadly defined standards. Individuals could marry whomever they wanted, as long as both parties had reached the requisite age and as long as their relationship did not come within the definition of the incestuous. Moreover, people could have only one spouse, as the state had adopted the religious norm of monogamy. Social standards about whom to marry and when to marry shifted as social conditions changed over the centuries, from heavy involvement by the immediate family to the sole responsibility of the two persons about to get married, but it remained almost entirely in the private sphere. Likewise, the decision of a couple to have children, and the number of children they might have, were never regulated in the United States; those decisions were never the object of substantial public subsidies or financial disincentives. In addition, families in the United States have maintained full control over where they lived; the right to move from state to state has even been circumscribed with constitutional protection.[10] Finally, most elements of relationships within families—how spouses treat each other and how parents and chidlren interact—have remained outside the government's control, although criminal statutes are invoked in cases of extreme maltreatment of spouses and children.[11]

The growth of the public sector in the nineteenth and twentieth centuries, however, involved large extensions into traditional private family matters. In the United States, governments became more concerned with the treatment of children when middle-class native-born white protestants became distressed at the conditions under which some immigrant children lived at the turn of the twentieth century.[12] Their agitation led to laws which permitted courts to take children from abusive or neglectful parents and place them in orphanages or foster homes. Foster homes provided care at public expense under the supervision of a welfare agency. Likewise, laws increasingly imposed public regulations on the adoptive process of taking a child into another family.[13]

Another intrusion into family life came with the extension of public schooling to the entire population and the outlawing of child labor. Child-labor laws prohibited employers from using children in most jobs and deprived some families of an important source of income. Compulsory school laws forced families to send their children—both boys and girls—to school.[14] Other intrusions accompanied mandatory schooling, such as compulsory health examinations and vaccinations.

Likewise, the law had always regulated the transmission of property upon death. It guaranteed the widow a minimum proportion of her husband's estate out of a concern that she not become a burden on public welfare.

The extent of today's intrusion by public law into family life, however, is not the consequence of conscious political decisions to regulate families more closely. Rather, it is the result of the increasing use of divorce, which had been available as a legal remedy for most of the history of the United States.

While government had little to say about whom and when to marry, its regulations about how one might divorce became pertinent to an increasing number of people. Arcane rules drew urgent attention from husbands and wives desperate to end their marriages. When the law failed to keep pace with the demand for divorces, couples sometimes resorted to fiction and fraud to satisfy the law's requirements. In New York, as we shall see, an entire cottage industry sprang up to produce fraudulent evidence of adultery in order to meet the requirements of that state's archaic law, which permitted divorce only upon showing of adultery as late as 1966. In other states, couples were carefully prompted to say the correct words in court to substantiate allegations of mental or physical cruelty.

The increasing popularity of divorce enlarged the involvement of civil law with family affairs. While civil law was silent about when a couple might marry, it provided stringent regulations about how long warring spouses had to wait until they could obtain a divorce. The marriage ritual was largely a function of religious or personal choice, but law and court rules dictated the divorce ceremony. Marriage was performed by the clergy of the couple's choice or by a judge of their choosing; when divorcing, a couple had little discretion in the choice of the judge who finalized their separation.

In the same way, the law of divorce intruded into family decisions about children and property. As long as marriages remained whole, parental supervision of children and spouses' decisions about property were beyond the scope of the law except in extreme cases of abuse. As soon as a couple divorced, these matters came under the routine scrutiny of public officials. A judge, who was a complete stranger to the family, habitually decided with whom the children should live unless the couple could make their own arrangement—and even such private arrangements were subject to judicial scrutiny. The same intrusion occurred with respect to property. In whole marriages, husbands and wives enjoyed enormous discretion over how they managed their finances. That freedom became severely circumscribed once they decided to divorce. The minimum amount that they set aside for the support of their children became the object of regulations issued by legislatures or courts. The amount they set aside for each other's subsistence also fell within the courts' jurisdiction. No property could be sold during a divorce proceeding without mutual consent or court approval. In extreme cases where couples could not agree upon how to divide their belongings, the judge, again a complete stranger, decided what belonged to each; this involved such large issues as the allocation of houses and apartments and the distribution of such trivia as carpets and cutlery.

The new laws of divorce which states adopted after 1965 increased public intrusion into family life, often inadvertently. The new divorce laws made divorce easier, but they imposed external norms on how divorced couples continued to relate to each other and to their children. For instance, parents had no obligation to send their children to college if their marriage was intact; in some states, however, support for a college education might be mandated for the children of divorced parents who could afford it.[15] Likewise, divorced parents with custody of their children might find it necessary to obtain court approval for a move to a new locale because that would affect the child's contact with the noncustodial parent; the criterion for approving such a move was often not the best interests of the parent but the best interests of the children.[16]

How these changes came about seems a mystery if we examine it through the perspective of our conventional understanding of politics. Policy change, especially of the magnitude of the alterations of divorce law, are supposedly the product of controversy and conflict, of a mass movement or of vigorous interest-group activity as recorded by the media. Yet little of this accompanied the reform of divorce law. To understand the success of divorce reform, we need to expand conventional concepts of policy formation.

There is a large discrepancy between conventional social-science models of policy making and observed instances. While policy analysts usually describe policy making as a task requiring almost herculean efforts to overcome immense barriers, a keen observer of the legislative scene writes, "The large majority of bills hold little interest for the legislators and are easily dispensed with."[17]

The barriers to policy making have been aptly described in numerous studies. New policies, it is said, originate in perceived performance gaps such as high crime rates,[18] extensive poverty,[19] or environmental hazards. They require the perception of resource slack so that they can be funded and administered without cutting other programs.[20] They must overcome the fragmentation of decision arenas where divisions between national and state/local institutions, conflict between contending houses of bicameral legislatures, rivalry of executive toward legislative institutions, and competition between contending agencies create a formidable obstacle course.[21] Finally, policy alternatives face overcrowded agendas, where proposals must utilize fleetingly open policy windows and seize upon an almost accidental coincidence of favorable circumstances in order to succeed.[22]

To overcome such hurdles, proposals must be driven by powerful forces according to accepted policy-making models. Several alternatives have been offered. To push their way through this forbidding maze, proposals are driven by social movements, as exemplified by the campaigns to enact the Civil

Rights Acts of the 1960s and to ratify the ERA. The former was the product of the civil rights movement,[23] and the latter was the object of the new feminist movement.[24] Alternatively, analysts point to vigorous interest-group activity[25] or guidance by extraordinarily crafty policy entrepreneurs[26] to explain the success of a legislative proposal.

Two explanations provide alternatives to this picture of a hyperactive policy arena. One is the aggregate-conditions model, which largely ignores the dynamics of the policy process and simply sets the conditions (usually in terms of performance gaps and resource slack) which accompany policy change.[27] The second is March and Olsen's[28] solutions-looking-for-a-problem model, which is driven by experts seeking to apply available solutions to problems that coincidentally present themselves.

Together these models provide a picture of the policy arena as one filled with highly charged participants engaged in intense resource mobilization. This description is largely based on a large number of case studies of landmark legislation, and it undoubtedly accounts for many policy decisions. However, such models neglect routine, low-visibility policy making which occupies most of the observable world of policy making.

Since Rosenthal and Forth's[29] examination of the volume of state legislation, it has been widely recognized that state legislatures pass an enormous amount of legislation. The making of policy by passing a law is not a rare event; on the contrary, it is a deluge. Rosenthal and Forth showed that between 1963 and 1974 each state on the average approved 856 bills per biennium; even the most restrained state, Utah, enacted 232 laws every two years during this period.[30] Their findings are not the spurious result of their choice of dates. One may also go to the statute books of the states, an annual publication of all the laws passed by the legislature. Using these books as an indicator of legislative output, we find that statutory law has increased steadily since the mid-1940s until the biennium 1982–83, when it reached the level of 1.5 million words for the average state.[31]

One may demur that much of this statutory output involves routine legislation, such as the passage of the state's budget, but budgets are saturated with policy decisions. However, the pages of state Session Laws do include policy changes of no great note. For instance, in 1979 New Mexico passed a Ski Safety Act which defined the legal duties and responsibilities of skiers and ski operators and limited the liabilities of ski facilities;[32] it also decided to label glue sniffing a petty misdemeanor.[33] In the same year, Georgia provided a measure of consumer protection by requiring rebuilt or reconditioned motor vehicles to be marked as such when a title was issued.[34] In Florida, House Bill 933 in 1975 clarified the type and size of fishing net that could be used to take shrimp in one area of its Gulf coast,[35] while another law gave official recognition to high school equivalence diplomas.[36] None of these laws, nor most of the other several hundred bills adopted in any year by a legislature, represent highly controversial policy decisions. They are part of the routine flow of policy making that occupies much of the time of American legislatures.

To produce such a flow of routine policy decisions, legislatures must operate with fewer constraints than the conventional policy paradigms suggest. Agendas must be more expansive, the fragmentation of the legislature less burdensome, and the resource requirements less exacting than we commonly suppose. However, we need not presume that routine policy making operates in an entirely different setting than when landmark legislation is considered.

Let us label the conventional descriptions of the policy process as "conflictual" processes because they typically involve a high degree of political controversy. We shall call the second set a family of "routine" policy processes because ordinary bills are passed with little notice or dissent. Like conflictual processes, routine processes exist in a number of variants.[37]

Conflictual and routine policy processes are closely related. They have the same characteristics, but in markedly different quantities. Routine policy proposals traverse the same paths as landmark bills, but they encounter less resistance than their more visible counterparts. It is this circumstance that oils the routine policy processes. The differences are summarized in table 1.

One important difference is that those who seek to use the routine policy process define their proposals in as narrow terms as they can. They seek to minimize the advertised impact

Table 1. Characteristics of Routine and Conflictual Policy Making

Trait	Routine	Conflictual
Definition of Problem	Constricted	Expansive
Interest Group Participation	Narrow	Broad
Influence of Experts	Near-Monopoly	Share with Nonexperts
Compatibility with Existing Policies	High	Low
Perceived Risk and Uncertainty	Low	High
Perceived Legitimacy of Policy	Accepted	Disputed
Cost of Policy	Low/None	Substantial
Public Visibility	Very Low	High

of their bill rather than to inflate it. They follow this strategy because they are not soliciting coalition partners who might be attracted by an additional feature of their proposal. On the contrary, they seek to restrict consideration of their proposal to as narrow a set of interest-group participants as they can.

Such a strategy has additional implications. It tends to inflate the influence of experts because the issue is defined in technical rather than populist terms. Emphasizing its technical complexity, proponents justify the large role of experts because only professionals have sufficient understanding to design a proper bill.

In addition, users of the routine policy process usually seek to emphasize the compatibility of their proposal with existing law and practice. Instead of promoting their suggestions as radical innovations in the manner of computer salespersons, promoters of routine policy changes emphasize the incremental character of their suggestions. Such an emphasis has two additional advantages for users of the routine policy process. One is that their proposals gain legitimacy because they are not characterized as radical departures from existing policies. The second is that the perceived risk and uncertainty engendered by their proposed change is minimized.

Users of routine policy processes also tend to design their policies to be inexpensive or cost-free. Avoiding large public or private expenditures enables advocates of such policies to avoid arousing potential opposition. No funds need to be taken from ongoing programs and no new taxes need to be imposed.

Finally, users of the routine policy process avoid media attention. Since they are not seeking widespread popular support and because they do not wish to arouse conflict, they adapt themselves to operating in the deep shadows of the political arena. Having defined their proposals narrowly, emphasized their technical complexity, and avoided large expenditures, advocates of such policies do not find it difficult to avoid media attention because the media find their activities and proposals uninteresting.

The preference of routine policy process for the shade resembles Cobb, Ross, and Ross's inside access model,[38] except that it does not depend on public officials or outsiders with extraordinary access to decision makers. Routine legislation often avoids the public agenda, while conflictual policy making depends upon it. Burstein, for instance, shows the importance of public opinion to the passage of OEO legislation,[39] as have Cobb et al. in their discussion of the public agenda.[40] In contrast, routine policy advocates do not seek public support; their strategy is to narrow issue definition and to restrict decisional participation because they often lack the resources to generate substantial public support.

When routine policy alterations surface in the form of legislative proposals, a consensus has already been built around a preferred solution in a manner to minimize controversy. As Nelson notes with respect to the child abuse legislation that swept through the states, "at each point when child abuse achieved a governmental agenda, the narrow definition was emphasized."[41] Such a narrow definition is achieved by clothing proposals in real or pseudo-technical complexity in order to exclude "outsiders" from its consideration, because the more limited the circle of participants in the policy process, the easier it is to manage.

It is essential to emphasize that the difference between routine policy making and its better known cousin, conflictual policy making, is one of degree, not kind. Indeed, routine policy making is often little more than the mirror image of the conflictual model. Both require resource mobilization, but routine policy alterations are usually designed to minimize that requirement, often by avoiding potential opposition. Both may benefit from social movement activity, but conflictual legislation is likely to be the specific target of a social movement, whereas routine legislation is likely to benefit from the wake of movement activity. Both are the beneficiary of the skills of policy entrepreneurs, but routine policy making requires fewer such skills and bestows less public recognition upon the successful entrepreneur. Both must overcome competition for public resources, but routine policy making often makes more modest demands on the public treasury than does landmark legislation. Both need to find a place on the formal agenda; conflictual bills do so because sufficient public interest has been generated to push the item onto a committee docket, but routine policy proposals find their way onto the agenda because agendas have to be filled with accomplishments as well as struggles, and easy bills are welcomed by committee chairs. Conflictual policy making often involves proposals advertised as dramatic departures from past practice, while routine policy making proposals promise little incompatibility with the past and emphasize their incremental nature. Consequently, decision makers are less concerned with risk and uncertainty in routine decision making.

Thus there is no single distinctive feature to routine policy making. Rather than belonging to a different genre, it generally consists of *much less* of the same characteristics as the conflictual policy making processes with which we are already familiar. It typically depends on the slow development of consensus that is accumulated through pre-legislative consultation among interested parties. The meetings involve interest groups, middle-level officials, and legislators (who may be back-benchers). Routine policy processes often include private citizens who have insinuated themselves into the process, perhaps because of their expertise or because of their insistence that a policy be changed, though without making a great public cause of it. Not all these intermediaries are necessary, because in some cases resistance to change may be very low for various reasons: the proposed policy may have low salience to many legislators; it may be seen as inevitable because of a federal or judicial mandate; it may appear to be little more than a minor increment to existing policy; or it may be perceived as the right thing to do to keep up with the times. In such instances, adoption is relatively easy although far from automatic. Moreover, although bureaucrats may be the originators of many routine policy changes, bureaucratic involvement is not a necessary prerequisite for change to be accepted. If we were to look for a single distinguishing factor, all of these differences appear to be summed up by the fact that routine policy change does not require the herculean efforts that the conventional models of policy making imply.

These characteristics of routine policy making give policy development the appearance of being a casual activity; they make it appear to be almost accidental. However, we shall see that the alteration of divorce law involved much activity, even though it attained little visibility or prominence. It encompassed both the strengths and weaknesses of routine policy making. It was neither accidental nor inevitable.

2

Social Conditions and Family Change

The legal revolution described in the previous chapter required
a supportive social, economic, and cultural context. While the
exact time at which the legal changes occurred and the precise
form they took were the result of the political forces which I
will describe in later chapters, the changes became possible
because of an altered social and economic environment in
which families found themselves in the last half of the twentieth century. Therefore, before turning to the politics of
divorce law revision, we need to understand the social and
economic context which nurtured those changes.

The conditions confronting husbands, wives, fathers, mothers, and children in the 1980s differ radically from those which
had faced their grandparents and great-grandparents. Both the
demography of the United Stated population and the labor
force participation of women have changed fundamentally.
Those changes together with others generated altered expectations about marriage, children, and the life course that people
could pursue.

Demographic Changes

Perhaps the most important change affecting American families was the continual lengthening of most Americans' life
spans. In 1900 women could expect to live only 48 years; in
1980, their expected life span had become almost 78 years.[1] In
part this was due to the lower mortality rate at childbirth, but it
was also the result of the general rise in the standard of living

that Americans experienced during those years. At the same time, married women began childbearing at a later age, families had fewer children, and more children survived to adulthood. Thus, 38% of all married women born between 1900 and 1904 had three or more children; in 1980, only 29.2% of white women and 36.4% of black women 18–34 years old expected three or more children during their lifetime.[2] Moreover, almost 30% of the women who were born between 1935 and 1944 and matured in the 1950s had their first child by the age of 20; less than one-quarter of their younger sisters born between 1950 and 1954 had their first child by that age.[3]

Even though childbearing began later for many, the longer life span meant that in 1980 most mothers could expect a very long period of active life after their children were grown, whereas in 1900 many women had not survived their children's adolescence. The increase in the male life span was almost as great. One consequence was that very few children became orphans in the 1980s and orphanages vanished from the social landscape. Another was that while in the early part of the century parents spent most of their adult lives with their young children, by the 1980s they could expect to have many years with an empty nest.

Finally, fewer men and women got married. Between 1960 and 1980, the percentage of never-married single adults increased by six points so that 23.8% of the male population and 17.1% of the female population remained unmarried in the 1980s.[4] At the same time, an increasing number of men and women were living together without being married, their number more than tripling between 1970 and 1981.[5] Thus marriage became somewhat less the expected norm for all young people.

Labor Market Changes

Participation by women in the labor force added momentum to transformation of American society begun by the demographic changes. During the first half of the century, most married women stayed at home; in 1900, only 5.6% of those married worked outside the home; by 1940 that had risen only to

13.8%. Thereafter, however, labor market participation of married women exploded with a rise of ten percentage points every decade.[6] By 1985, 54.3% of all married women were in the labor force.[7] Indeed, by 1985 a majority of married mothers with infants under three years old were working.[8] In addition, more of these women worked continuously just like their husbands, forsaking the intermittent employment pattern of their mothers and grandmothers. Moreover, women entered a much larger range of occupations by the 1980s than they had at the beginning of the century. Women became fire fighters, police officers, truckers, plumbers, and carpenters as well as lawyers, judges, doctors, and scientists. Women remained a small minority in high-status occupations, but their numbers indicated that occupational barriers against women were crumbling. Because most women worked as secretaries, school teachers, beauticians, and other occupations that had traditionally been set aside for them and which were assigned lower wages, their incomes remained lower than men's. Other factors also contributed to the lower income of women. One was their pattern of more intermittent participation in the labor force than men; another was their later entry into career ladders; a third was a pattern of wage discrimination based on the traditional view that women did not need a "family wage" while men did. On the average, by the 1980s, women's wages remained only 70% of the earnings of men. However, the number of women in executive and managerial positions increased markedly in the 1970s, so that by the end of the decade 30.5% of all workers in those categories were women.[9] The result was that more high-salaried positions became available to a minority of women, allowing a small number to earn sizeable incomes which were almost unheard-of in earlier years.

These changes transformed almost every dimension of family life in the United States. They began to erode women's dependence upon men for their living; an increasing number of women began to believe that earning their own living was a viable alternative to economic security through marriage. While it may be true that such perceptions outstripped reality, because most women continued to earn too little to support themselves (or their children) well, economic barriers against divorce seemed much less formidable by 1980s than in any prior period of American history.

The wage-earning role of women placed great stress on working wives because many husbands expected their wives to manage the home in addition to working a full-time job. Bianchi and Spain summarize the available research as follows: "Regardless of the sample or methodology used, every study to date on the household division of labor has found that women perform more household tasks than men. This relationship applies to couples in which the wife works full time and those in which she works part time or not at all."[10] Even when husbands shared such household chores as grocery shopping, laundry, vacuuming, and cooking, family life often was stressful. Such a blurring of traditional gender roles generated considerable tension in some marriages because of the unaccustomed role in which men found themselves. Unlike their fathers, who had been family patriarchs, an increasing number of husband found themselves to be no more than equal partners in the family enterprise. All of these factors combined to increase the probability of divorce for working wives over that for wives who stayed at home.[11]

The full-time work of wives also changed household economies. Many working-class and middle-class families became accustomed to a standard of living that was attainable only with two incomes. Families could not afford single family houses, two cars, electronic entertainment centers, or family vacations without the wife's "extra" earnings. The change between 1960 and 1980 was a dramatic one. In 1960, 60% of all wives contributed no cash earnings to the household economy; twenty years later, that proportion had dwindled to less than 40%. On the other hand, while fewer than two in ten wives earned over 30% of the family's income in 1960, by 1980 more than three in ten did so.[12] Thus, while women became less dependent on men for their livelihood, they and their husbands became more tied to the revenues generated by joint incomes if they were to maintain their standard of living.

Full-time work for mothers also changed childrearing. Child-care facilities, whether they were individual baby-sitters or play-school nurseries, became the primary caretakers of the children of many American working mothers. Between 1958 and 1982, the proportion of mothers using child care outside their home while working full time leaped from 31.6% to 62%.[13] Schooling had long since become near-universal until the age of 16 or 18, hence some children from as early an age as one spent their weekdays outside home except to eat breakfast and dinner and to sleep at night.

The labor market also changed for men and children. For children the change came early in the century with their exclusion from the labor force. Child labor was effectively outlawed by 1938 under the Fair Labor Standards Act, after which children worked mostly at odd jobs especially reserved for them such as newspaper delivery. That had a dramatic impact, as Zelizer argues, on how society perceived the worth of children.[14] They became valueless, in the sense that they ceased to contribute to the economic well-being of the family. At the same time the costs of childrearing increased, particularly with the expectation of many more years of schooling and dependency. Yet children were far from being regarded as worthless; indeed, the opposite may have been the case for they moved from being valued as economic assets toward being perceived as priceless in terms of their companionship. It is telling that couples who could not have children were willing to pay large sums of money for the privilege of adopting a child[15] or having a child through a surrogate. Children became pals for their parents. As one television news commentator put it in the early 1980s in referring to the children of the baby-boom generation, they were "yuppie-puppies." Thus children came to be valued by many principally for their companionship rather than for the economic contribution they might make.

That was true even during parents' old age. In earlier periods, parents expected their children to help during their waning years, but the conditions of work and governmental policy substituted an institutionalized welfare system and pensions for most Americans. In addition, a decreasing proportion of the elderly lived with their children and resided in segregated communities of the elderly or in nursing homes instead. Thus the value of children became transformed and their economic worth became insignificant for many.

The change in the labor market for men occurred later than

for children and women and had more subtle consequences. One change was the obverse of that occurring for women: men more frequently found themselves working side-by-side with women and occasionally under their supervision. These conditions created a relationship outside marriage that was quite different than that which had confronted their fathers, and they further created a whole new set of employment grievances over sexual harassment by men in the work place. The entry of women into the work force also enlarged the labor force and contributed to the downward pressure on the pay of American workers, because women continued to be paid less than their male counterparts in most occupations. For a variety of reasons, many American workers in the late 1970s found themselves confronted with pay cuts rather than raises, while employers abandoned all pretense of paying a "family wage" which would permit men to support their families without a second wage earner. In some industries unions were forced to agree to wage cuts in order to save jobs; in others, workers had to settle for lower paid work after being laid off by their former employer and finding new jobs in lower paying occupations.

The consequence was that as women were coming to feel more empowered and less dependent, many men were experiencing the opposite. Not only did they have to accommodate themselves to wives who worked and who earned a large share of the family's income, but they also had to recognize that their own earning power and authority had diminished.[16] Increasingly, they answered to a woman as boss on the job and to a wife as co-equal at home. That was a large step from the patriarchal household in which most men had grown up, one which had been idealized in the following terms:

From the corroding cares of business, from the hard toil and frequent disappointments of the day, men retreat to the bosoms of their families, and there, in the midst of that sweet society of wife and children and friends, receive a rich reward for their industry. . .[17]

The Effects of Feminism

The feminist movement has been another potent promoter of change in family life during the latter half of the twentieth century. Beginning in the early 1960s, feminism once again became a visible and articulate voice on the American scene. Its revival was closely related to the success of the civil rights movement in mobilizing minorities; women perceived themselves in a parallel position. The first moves toward mobilizing women came from the Kennedy administration through its President's Conference on the Status of Women, which received much support from the Women's Bureau in the Department of Labor.[18] The National Organization for Women developed as a response to the conference and its successors.[19]

Both the governmental organizations and the National Organization for Women immediately focused on labor market problems of women. Discrimination on account of sex had been outlawed under Title VII of the Civil Rights Act of 1964, partly as a maneuver by conservatives to kill the entire bill,[20] but instead of succeeding, the tactic expanded the law immensely. Moreover, other federal enactments outlawed wage discrimination. Consequently, a legal basis developed for seeking to end gender discrimination at the workplace, a goal that was perceived to be crucial in the struggle of women for social equality. At the same time, the activities of the feminist movement bolstered the already existing shift of women into paid work. The two reinforced one another.

A second major thrust of the feminist movement was its campaign for the Equal Rights Amendment, which centered on the theme that women were the political, economic, and social equals of men. The amendment was to outlaw unequal treatment of women wherever it occurred. It was particularly expected to affect the legal system's treatment of women in such areas as criminal law, labor law, property rights, and family law. Even though it failed ratification, it focused much attention on residual discrimination against women in a wide variety of contexts.

One of those contexts provided an additional focus for feminist activity: the manner in which women were treated as victims of physical assault and abuse. Feminists were appalled at the way in which the police and courts often treated rape victims as if they were co-defendants. Similarly, they were dismayed at the tendency of law enforcement officials to minimize incidents of wife abuse and incest (which often involved daughters). Throughout the country, local activists established rape crisis centers and shelters for abused women.[21] They then turned to political activity to change the laws and the operation of the police and courts so that victimized women would receive more sympathetic treatment and offenders would be punished.[22] Consequently, law enforcement officials increasingly intervened in family disputes and imposed legal constraints upon offending men.

The impact of these activities on families was usually diffuse rather than direct. As we shall see in the following chapters, family law itself was not a high priority on NOW's agenda; most resources were directed toward ratification of ERA and toward working at the federal level for implementation of the anti-discrimination legislation that already existed.[23]

However, the rhetoric of the feminist movement did not fall on deaf ears and had an enormous impact on the ways in which many Americans conceptualized the ideal family structure. Talk of marriage as a contract between equals became more common and undermined the traditional view of marriage as a special relationship in which the husband dominated by natural right. The new view of marriage as a bond between equals had many consequences, including justifying a wife's claim to retain her maiden name, her choice of where she would live, and her right to decide whether she would work outside the home.

Feminist rhetoric about marriage as a partnership of equals also helped undermine conventional task assignments within the family according to gender. Women, according to feminists, did not have to feel guilty if they shared childrearing tasks, and men ought not consider such tasks as changing a diaper or feeding a child as demeaning to their masculinity. Feminism thus helped legitimate the crumbling of distinctive gender roles that was already being fostered by the increased labor force participation of women.

Feminist ideas also encouraged women to think of themselves as responsible for their own economic well-being. Feminists argued that it was right that women support themselves and that the labor market should change so that they could do so adequately. It was anathema to feminists for the law to treat ex-wives as incompetents who could not care for themselves. Most feminists in the 1960s and 1970s did not perceive any problem with transforming alimony (which presumed a continuing obligation of a husband to support his ex-wife until another man took up the responsibility) into a temporary and transitional maintenance payment, designed to allow a woman to take up the responsibility of caring for herself independently.

Thus the feminist movement had a profound, although indirect, impact on ideals of marriage. It legitimated new ways of thinking about the family relationships which were already changing as a result of demographic and labor market forces. For some persons, prescription and description became confused. Feminists, of course, argued that women ought to be treated as equals but were in fact often the victims of discrimination. Others, however, heard the message differently and began to act as if women were already equal to men in every respect. That attitude was reflected in such trivial matters as social etiquette: "ladies first" became a less frequently invoked rule and men less commonly gave up their seats to women on buses and rapid transit trains or held doors open for them when they entered buildings. As we shall see, assumptions about women's equality also played a large role in new legal rules about alimony, child support, and property division after marriage.

Normative Changes in Family Life

Conventional expectations about marriage centered around three alternative marriage styles.[24] One perceived marriage as centering on conceiving and raising children. A second presumed that the family was a primary economic unit through which husbands and wives contributed to their collective welfare by performing specialized tasks. Finally, marriage could be perceived as providing long-term companionship for husbands and wives; they married principally because they loved each other and enjoyed each other's companionship.

These three models rarely existed in pure form. Most husbands and wives throughout the twentieth century would have subscribed to several or all of them if asked about their family ideals. However, modal expectations about marriage clearly changed during the past eighty years.

Child-centered marriages were more common at the turn of the century than in the 1980s for many reasons. Some we have already located in the demographic and labor market changes that occurred during this period. But others were also important. The invention of the contraceptive pill had a profound impact on sexual mores. For the first time in human history, it seemed possible to separate sexual activity from the probability of procreation. In addition, abortion was legalized by the 1973 Supreme Court decision of *Roe v. Wade*. Recreational sex outside the confines of a bordello became attainable and was openly discussed as laudable in some circles. Many married couples no longer felt that sexual intimacy need result in conception. If survey information on such matters is to be believed, an increasing proportion of the population became tolerant of premarital sex; whereas 68% thought it wrong in 1969, only 39% found it objectionable in 1985.[25] Many people no longer saw marriage as the only acceptable context for sexual activity, nor did they accept having children as the inevitable consequence of sex. Indeed, by the middle 1980s more marriages were childless than before, as more husbands and wives postponed having children or decided against it entirely.

Marriage as an economic base also became transformed, as we have already seen. The family had ceased to be a unit of production with the industrialization of the United States. The labor market changes of the twentieth century eroded the gender based specialization of tasks within the family. However, as we have already noted, husband-wife combinations acquired a new economic significance when dual incomes became necessary to support middle-class life-styles. Although marriage is not often thought of in economic terms as it had been in earlier times, its economic component remains salient to many.

The companionate marriage style has become dominant.[26] The romantic ideal not only rules courtship, but it also governs the criteria for continuing marriages. The life span of most Americans produces a prolonged period during which marriages can persist. For most of that time, as we have already indicated, children are not present to focus affection and activity. But in addition, the life style of urban Americans throws husbands and wives together more than in earlier times. In-laws, siblings, and cousins more often live in different neighborhoods or different cities than that of the husband and wife. Neither can find refuge with a nurturing relative as easily as before. The bar, the movie theater, and even the ball park have been largely replaced by television, so that people spend more of their free time at home than before. Finally, husbands and wives have more free time. The standard work week has become five days so that many have the weekend entirely free from work. The workday is usually only eight hours, leaving evenings free from obligatory activities.

In these circumstances, marriages which are not companionate quickly become intolerable. Intolerable marriages more frequently lead to divorce and alternative life-styles appear viable.

One alternative is to seek the companionship of another man or woman. In the early part of the century, both men and women had few contacts with those of the opposite sex other than their kin. Men mostly worked with other men; women stayed at home and visited with other women. By the 1980s that had changed, so that many men came into contact with women other than their wives at their work, and most women who worked came into contact with men other than their husbands. The increased contact between men and women at their workplace undoubtedly accounts for the increased prominence of sexual harassment incidents. But in addition, the increased contact brought men and women together in situations which could lead to friendship and alternatives to companionship within an existing marriage.

Moreover, the moral imperative of lifetime marriage had become undermined. Divorce in the minds of many was transformed from an act of immorality to a symptom of social illness. The remedy was not to punish or to persist in what religion prescribed. Rather, unhappiness resulting from an unsatisfying marriage was perceived as an infirmity that could be either treated with psychotherapy or excised by divorce. The perception of marital unhappiness as a condition to be assuaged rather than one to be abhorred grew gradually in tandem with the broader redefinition of mental illness and social maladjustments. It contributed to legitimizing divorce because divorce was seen as one of several alternative effective treatments.[27]

In addition, divorce became legitimized by its increasing use throughout the population. In the early part of the century, it was a rarity associated with scandal. To be divorced, particulary for women, was severely stigmatizing, unless one were an entertainer where the stigma added to an artist's mystique. After World War II, however, the divorce rate, which had been dampened through the Great Depression and the war, resumed its gradual rise and briefly accelerated. By the 1970s, for the first time in American history more marriages were dissolved through divorce than by the death of one of the spouses.[28] It was widely predicted that half of all marriages begun in the 1970s would end in divorce.[29] On a personal level, many people began to have direct experience with divorce in the 1970s, either with the dissolution of their own marriage or that of relatives, friends, and acquaintances, and those experiences lessened the social sting of divorce. It became almost as commonplace as marriage.

In addition, religious impediments to divorce weakened. While never encouraged by mainstream denominations, the opposition which some had expressed diminished. That was especially apparent with the Catholic Church. While it continued to regard marriage as a lifelong sacrament, annulments became easier to obtain and divorced parishioners became the object of special attention rather than simple condemnation. Divorce rates among Catholics continued to be lower than among Protestants, but divorce was no longer universally condemned.

Conclusion

These social and economic changes altered the context of married life in the United States. The marriage vow, "until death do us part," had new meaning when life extended almost twice as long in the 1980s as in the 1900s. The long period without children and the financial contribution of women modified relationships between wives and husbands. Husbands could no longer automatically claim autocratic dominance and wives more often sought a greater degree of equality. Most significantly, however, the focus of marriages shifted from children and economics to companionship.

Many of these changes occurred in other industrialized nations of the West at about the same time as in the United States:[30] labor force participation of women increased during the twentieth century and the life expectancy of adults became much longer. Families had fewer children, and the obligation of supporting aged parents was transferred even earlier than in the United States from the private to the public sector through social insurance programs. Contraception became widely available in Western Europe at about the same time as in the United States. These trends were not identical in all nations, but their direction was the same. It was therefore no accident that many West European nations revised their divorce laws at about the same time as the United States did.

The changes we have described were not anti-family. Many of the divorced remained in contact with their children, in-laws, and ex-spouses. Those who escaped from their existing marriages often entered new ones within a few years. By the last decades of the century, serial marriages and blended families had become more common; but one must remember that a century earlier, many widows and widowers had also been involved in similar marriage patterns. Thus family life did not necessarily decline but rather changed.

The changes in family life encouraged many to consider alternatives to remaining in their first marriage. With neither children nor economic benefit looming as large as the desire for companionship in the later years of the twentieth century, marriages which did not provide companionship were more readily seen as dispensable. Public opinion polls reflect the change in that sentiment. In 1936 a Gallup poll indicated that three-quarters of the sample opposed liberalizing divorce laws; even in New York, where divorce could be obtained only on the allegation of adultery, a bare 51% supported change. As late as 1966, only 13% of Gallup's sample thought divorce laws too strict. Yet by 1974, even after a majority of states had already adopted no-fault divorce, a third of a national sample thought divorce should be made still easier to obtain.[31]

Thus, altered social conditions nurtured changed attitudes and expectations about marriage. With many chafing in marriages which threatened to persist much longer than most people remembered their parents' or grandparents' marriages enduring under laws that were widely considered overly restrictive, it became easy for legislatures to consider revising divorce laws. It did not make revision inevitable, nor did changed social conditions dictate the precise form of the changes. Those were the product of the particular political forces which I shall describe in the following chapters.

3

Breaking the Logjam of Divorce Law Revision: New York

The first successful effort to change the basic provisions of divorce laws in the United States in the mid-twentieth century occurred in New York. That was no accident. New York had the nation's most restrictive divorce law despite the state's reputation for liberalism and cosmopolitanism. New York's reform, however, was far from radical. It did no more than bring the state's laws into the twentieth century.

The Historical Context of Reform

In 1966 New York's law permitted divorce only upon demonstration of adultery. It was penned by Alexander Hamilton, who in 1787 authored the law to provide a general procedure by which divorce could be dispensed by the courts instead of having the legislature grant each and every divorce. Through a series of historical vagaries, the law was not amended before the Civil War, when most of the other states liberalized their divorce codes to include physical and mental cruelty among other grounds for ending a marriage. Moreover, New York's law did not lend itself to liberalization through court interpretation, as was the case in other states, because New York's adultery provision left little room for embellishment. When immigration swelled the number of Roman Catholics in New York and boosted the political power of the church in the last decades of the nineteenth century, the old law became more firmly entrenched. A combination of conservative upstate Republicans, who often controlled the legislature and its key committees, and urban Democrats, who were responsive to the Catholic sensitivities of their constituents, made divorce law reform an unlikely project for entrepreneurial politicians. In addition, New Yorkers had no model of daring innovation in family law elsewhere in the nation. The most important legal changes in the domestic status of women had occurred in the mid-nineteenth century, when the Married Women's Property Acts were passed to permit women to own and control their own property. New York had adopted one of the more far-reaching of these laws, but its passage was not motivated by a desire to alter the essentials of family relationships. Moreover, it was interpreted in a quite conservative manner by New York's judges.[1]

Another legal change adopted elsewhere as early as the 1930s affected divorce more directly but not fundamentally. Several states experimented with requiring or offering conciliation procedures before divorce could be granted. Sponsors of such laws saw conciliation as a means of preventing hasty divorces and saving marriages which might otherwise end. The programs, however, cost considerable money, and many people questioned their efficacy, particularly if they relied on clients to volunteer for their services, because such a procedure self-selected the couples most likely to respond to last-ditch efforts to save their marriage;[2] compulsory conciliation threatened to cost still more.

Efforts to require conciliation before divorce reflected two of the dominant perceptions of divorce. The first, which was particularly representative of nineteenth-century views, perceived divorce in terms of the moral importance of maintaining families intact. Divorce was condemned in religious terms as an unmitigated evil and its spread was a cause for alarm. For instance, in 1828, Timothy Dwight, president of Yale University, bemoaned the rapid spread of divorce in the following terms:

At the present time, the progress of this evil is alarming and terrible. In this town [New Haven], within five years, more than fifty divorces have been granted; at the average calculation, more than four hundred in the whole state during this period . . ."[3]

Similar sentiments were expressed by Horace Greeley at mid-century,[4] and at the end of the century they were at the core of the National Divorce Reform League, renamed in 1897 as the National League for the Protection of the Family.[5] That organization was able to capitalize on renewed concern about the evil of divorce and lobbied state legislatures to tighten their laws. As a consequence, many other states amended their laws by adding restrictive provisions, but New York's remained the same since it had never liberalized divorce.[6] The moralistic view of divorce which motivated the stricter divorce laws of the early twentieth century later resonated in the endeavor to establish conciliation procedures in the belief that every effort should be made to save faltering marriages.

The conciliation procedures adopted in the twentieth century also reflected a newer psychiatric view of marital breakdown. In this view, divorce did not reflect evil but a psychological disorder that could be treated through therapy. Poor marital relations, in this view, were a sign of ill mental health that could be cured or ameliorated by making wives and husbands more cognizant of the deeper psychological problems reflected by their marital disputes. Hence, counseling seemed a suitable response to marital stress.[7]

Quite a different reaction to divorce came from the courts. While legislatures narrowed the provisions of statutory law and in a few states ordered conciliation, many courts faced with a rising wave of divorce petitions interpreted their procedural codes leniently and granted divorce without testing the evidence offered in support of the petition. By the turn of the century, divorce law had taken the form of strict black-letter law modified by lenient court practice, so that in most states divorce could be obtained more easily than the words of the statutes suggested.[8] That allowed legislators to resist change and speak for morality because they knew that the courts did not interpret the statutes they adopted in a literal way.

The Crystallization of Reform

Divorce reform was slow to come to New York, but when it did, it succeeded with much less effort than its past history would have suggested. In retrospect, many of those involved in the effort thought it went so easily because "the time was ripe," but that phrase disguises specific political developments that

often occur in routine policy making. Divorce reform succeeded so easily because it was removed from the center of
political controversy by a set of fortuitous events. It then
passed without generating strong opposition. Ironically, the
low-keyed success of the reform prevented its principal sponsor from using it as a platform for political advancement. It
was a textbook example of routine policy making.

Framing the Issue

Proponents of divorce reform in New York did not mount a
frontal assault on the old law on behalf of a radical cause such
as feminism or alternative life styles. Neither played a discernible role. Feminism asserted no influence because the new
feminist movement had not yet organized in the early 1960s
when divorce reform was being promoted in New York. Alternative life-styles were not the issue because New York was not
California and in the early 1960s the alternative life style most
prominent was that of "hippies," whose long hair, loose sex,
and drug-induced euphoria were politically more a hazard
than an asset.

Divorce reform in New York was presented in much less
controversial terms as a necessary *procedural* alteration. Reformers focused on the disjunction between law-on-the-books
and law-in-action. They argued that the rigor of the black letter
law cultivated corruption in divorce courts because judges
were presented with fraudulent divorce petitions. Lenient
court interpretations of the evidence supporting divorce petitions had made divorce available to those willing to bend the
truth, although the truth often needed to be twisted beyond all
recognition in order to satisfy the statutory requirement for
proof of adultery. Consequently, the proof was often manufac-
tured. As early as the last third of the nineteenth century,
purists had complained about the fraud perpetrated on the
courts. Nelson Blake, a historian of New York's divorce laws,
described such criticism in the following terms:

As early as 1869, the NEW YORK TIMES was condemning the
'trade' in procurement of divorce 'by means of fraud and perjury.'
Evidence given on the nature of the longstanding problem is: a professional perjurer in divorce cases who was sent to jail for 9 years in

1870; a deputy clerk in Brooklyn court who was accused for having forged some 50 fraudulent divorce decrees in 1884; and a 1934 feature in the NEW YORK MIRROR of a sensational series entitled 'I was the Unknown Blond in 100 New York Divorces!'[9]

In the early 1960s a sociologist found the same conditions still existing and cited the following words of a New York matrimonial lawyer as typical of the situation: "The amount of perjury is terrible. I know it; the judges know it; we all know it."[10] The way to eliminate this abuse, according to the reformers, was to make divorce available for reasons which would not require perjury.

This argument, of course, sidestepped the considerable evidence from the remainder of the country, where divorce was available on a variety of grounds but mostly procured on proof of "extreme mental cruelty"—as suspect as New York's adultery proofs although less lurid. Across the country, women uniformly complained of severe headaches or sleepless nights in response to the routine questioning of their attorneys. New York's reformers, however, did not investigate this problem because the procedural character of their proposals was an essential ruse to avoid debate on more fundamental issues about the character of family life under liberalized divorce rules.

Another element of the procedural argument in New York was the manner in which attorneys and clients evaded New York's divorce law by other strategms which seemed to undermine respect for the law. Two were commonly used. The first was to send clients to another state or country which had more lenient codes. The most popular destinations were Nevada and Mexico because they combined speed with sunny leisure. In Nevada, ranches existed whose sole purpose was to cater to divorce-bound clients and provide comfortable surroundings while the plaintiff met the state's six-week residency requirement. On the day the six-week period ended, the client walked into a nearby courtroom, got her[11] divorce, and returned to New York. The process was so well known that everyone knew that a book titled "The Road to Reno"[12] was about divorce. These migratory divorces, of course, were available only to the rich, but among the rich they were fashionable. As late as 1962, the wife of Governor Nelson Rockefeller obtained such a migratory divorce.

Annulments were the second evasive device. The grounds for annulment were slightly more generous than for divorce. A marriage could be annulled if the parties had been under eighteen when married, were incapable of consenting to marriage for lack of understanding, were physically impotent or frigid, had consented to marriage because of fraud or compulsion, or had been incurably insane for at least five years.[13] These provisions also invited fraud, but the stigma attached to the claim that the marriage had not been consummated was somewhat less than the claim of adultery needed for divorce. Moreover, New York's courts interpreted these provisions liberally, and judicial interpretation expanded the statutory grounds for annulment to dozens of analogous situations.[14] New York consequently had the highest annulment rate of the nation, accounting for as many as one-third of all annulments in the United States.[15]

The evasion and fraud associated with divorce and annulment in New York thus provided an issue which motivated some—especially elite lawyers—to work for change. The issue they posed was the threat that existing divorce laws posed to the integrity of New York's legal system.

The Avoidance of Controversy

Using the cover provided by procedural reform was not, however, sufficient. Earlier similar attempts to change New York's divorce law had failed because there was a strong consensus that divorce reform was politically too dangerous. Meddling with divorce laws threatened to provoke gloomy forecasts of social disaster because of the breakdown of family life occasioned by divorce; whatever the actual level of divorce, commentators like Timothy Dwight perceived it as perilous and rising at a menacing rate. A vote to liberalize the law made legislators vulnerable to the charge of promoting that dangerous trend.

Considerable experience reinforced that perception. In New York, the most formidable and vocal opponent to liberalization of its divorce laws was the Catholic church. It played a prominent role in defeating divorce reform bills from the mid-1930s through the 1950s. Whenever a bill to liberalize divorce came before the New York legislature, a representative of the Catholic Welfare League reminded lawmakers of the church's opposition.[16] The vigor of the church's opposition in the 1950s was recalled thirty years later by a matrimonial attorney. The lawyer remembered that when attorneys authored a report in the 1950s recommending extensive changes in New York's divorce law, they were told that they would be in trouble if they ever tried to run for elective office or faced a Catholic judge. They were advised by a Catholic friend to go to the office of the Archdiocese to straighten things out. They did so.[17]

However, in the early 1960s a series of events unrelated to family policy made it less likely that divorce reform would provoke such threats. They changed the landscape of New York politics.

One set of changes radically altered the New York legislature, which had been dominated by upstate legislators representing what were often staunchly conservative and Republican rural areas. The city was drastically underrepresented. That changed as the result of a U.S. Supreme Court decision in 1962 requiring state legislatures to be reapportioned to equalize the population of legislative districts.[18] The case originated in Tennessee but affected every state legislature. The districts from which representatives and senators were elected had to be remapped and new elections called. New York's reapportionment brought many more urban legislators to Albany and undermined the power of the upstate conservatives who had long helped block revision of New York's divorce code.

Two years later, Barry Goldwater ran his ill-fated campaign for the Presidency against Lyndon Johnson. Goldwater was crushed in New York and he carried to defeat some of the remaining conservative Republicans who had so long dominated New York's legislature. Those circumstances diluted the institutionalized power of the opposition to divorce revision.

Other events sapped the strength of Catholic opposition to more permissive divorce laws. Pope Pius XII died in 1958 and was replaced by John XXIII, who liberalized many aspects of Catholic life. After the Second Vatican Council which met between 1962 and 1965, the church streamlined its procedures for religious annulments and became less hostile to divorced people. Equally important for the course of divorce revision in New York was the waning influence of New York's Cardinal Spellman.[19] He had long taken an active role in New York politics and was a respected power broker in both the city and the state. His influence rested not only on his position as the highest Catholic prelate in the state, but also on his close ties to Pope Pius and his considerable personal vigor. However, he did not enjoy as close a relationship with the new pope as he had with Pius XII, and as he grew older and less energetic, his power ebbed and his political positions became more vulnerable. In addition, Spellman's duties as military vicar to American troops in Vietnam distracted him from local issues. Thus, by the mid-1960s Catholic opposition to divorce revision no longer appeared as insurmountable as it had in the past.

Still another fortuitous event conspired to reduce the controversial character of divorce reform. In 1962, New York reelected Nelson Rockefeller as governor, even though his wife had obtained an out-of-state divorce earlier that year. Governor Rockefeller's divorce and reelection had attracted wide attention as a signal that politicians no longer needed to fear divorce as a threat to their ambitions. The incident also was seen as a favorable omen among those seeking to change New York's divorce laws, for although Rockefeller studiously avoided public endorsement of divorce revision, the sponsors had little doubt that he would sign it.[20]

Thus several events combined to defuse controversy surrounding proposed changes in New York's divorce laws. The composition of the legislature was transformed; the long-standing opposition of the Catholic church waned as a consequence of Vatican II and the declining influence of Cardinal Spellman; and politicians learned that divorce had become less politically salient through the reelection of recently divorced Governor Rockefeller.

The Emergence of a Sponsor

Before reform could become a reality, it needed a champion. Chance produced such a sponsor in Jerome Wilson, a junior legislator and member of the reform wing of the Democratic party. He was not a lawyer; he had never before been concerned with New York's divorce law. He was not a member of the mental health community that Halem describes as being increasingly hospitable to no-fault divorce. Rather, he earned his living in public relations while going evenings to law school at New York University.

He embraced divorce reform on a challenge from a member of the editorial staff of the *New York Times*. As he described the birth of his interest, he was running for reelection and had failed to obtain the *Times*'s endorsement, although he had won backing from most of the other reform groups. In a fit of pique, he requested a meeting with a member of the editorial board of the *Times* and asked what he had done wrong. He was told that he had done nothing wrong, but that his name had not been attached to any accomplishment in Albany. The legislator then asked what the *Times*'s man would have him do. The editorialist listed three issues, one of which was divorce reform, and at that moment the legislator's interest in the issue was born.[21] Another not inconsistent account stresses equally coincidental circumstances. According to this second account, the legislator was at New York University one evening looking for his law professor, and not finding him, knocked on the next door. That office was occupied by one of the country's leading experts on family law. Upon learning that the student was a member of the state legislature, the professor berated him about New York's antiquated law and aroused his interest in changing it.[22]

The legislator fulfilled the pledge. He wanted to spark widespread interest in divorce reform in the hope that committee hearings and his subsequent sponsorship of the reform bill would attract sufficient attention to win him more prominence. He therefore staged a series of hearings across the state in the fall of 1965 that succeeded in receiving some attention from the media. However, the hearings did not spark controversy. They mostly heard testimony supporting the liberalization of New York's restrictive law, with emphasis on the painful experiences of persons denied divorce because they could not afford to go to Nevada and did not want to stage a fictitious adultery episode. The legislator scheduled the hearings in Albany, where he hoped for attention from his legislative colleagues, and in New York City and Buffalo, where media coverage might be obtained. Ironically, the _Times_ did not pay much attention to the hearings, but the _Herald Tribune_ printed a several-part series on divorce in New York.[23] It was enough publicity to successfully court fellow legislators and obtain an influential co-sponsor in the Assembly; it was not so much as to arouse spirited opposition from conservatives.

A second promoter of divorce reform worked to obtain the support of the elite Bar Association of the City of New York.[24] He was admiralty law specialist Howard Hilton Spellman (no relation to Cardinal Spellman), who chaired a special committee of the association on family law. Spellman and the Bar Association were also principally interested in ending the widespread fraud that divorce cases generated rather than making divorce more widely available. Howard Spellman's efforts brought the prestige of the legal elite to the cause of divorce law reform, although legislators considered him an ineffectual lobbyist.

Both the legislator and Spellman enlisted the services of Professor Henry H. Foster of New York University Law School. A nationally recognized expert in family law who brought additional prestige to the effort, Foster helped draft the legislation as well as the committee's report supporting it.[25] The report's emphasis was on the urgent need to eliminate fraud and perjury and to restore public confidence in the integrity of New York's divorce courts.

The fact that divorce would be substantially easier to obtain could scarcely be disguised, causing concern among legislators who remembered earlier unsuccessful efforts to liberalize New York's divorce laws. That concern, however, was ameliorated by the inclusion of compulsory conciliation proceedings, an idea long supported by Foster. The legislative hearings had paid some attention to conciliation; they obtained testimony from the Chief Judge of the Los Angeles Conciliation Court and from Foster. But perhaps the most dramatic testimony came accidentally. As the witness testified:

The board of directors' meeting for CARE brought me to New York City today. This morning, at the hotel, I turned on the television set and heard Hugh Downes interviewing Professor Henry Foster on the Today Show. I hurried to the shower and went over to NBC to see the professor. There I met your chairman, Senator Jerome Wilson, and, at his invitation, here I am to explain briefly the operation of the Family Court of Milwaukee.[26]

This judge's testimony was amply quoted in the committee's final report in support of including a similar provision in the New York bill.[27] That move proved to be tactically important because it disarmed critics who charged that the bill was anti-family.

The legislative history of the bill demonstrates the importance of skilled legislative sponsorship. At several points the bill seemed on the verge of being pigeonholed or defeated. This occurred despite the absence of organized opposition, as even the church's lobbyist was not visibly active. The bill was saved largely by the skillful maneuvering of its legislative sponsors, who had no interest-group backing other than that of the Bar Association of the City of New York. The legislative hearings which were held while the legislature had been adjourned sufficed to place the matter on the legislature's agenda, perhaps because it promised an attractive reform without the expenditure of extravagant effort. However, it was necessary to overcome the lack of enthusiasm of conservative Republicans who had not been the originators of the bill and who traditionally were suspicious of divorce liberalization. This was particularly important because by the time the bill came before the legislature, another election had been held and the Republicans had recaptured control of the Senate although not the Assembly. Thus, it was essential that the effort be bipartisan, which meant that the original Democratic sponsors had to accommodate the new Republican leadership. That was done both by revising the list of sponsors who would get credit for the legislation and by altering the details of the bill. The Republican leadership drafted its own version, which modified how long a couple needed to be separated before their separation could be converted into a divorce. Eventually, all those involved in the negotiations agreed upon a two-year period. The final bill thus included a number of grounds for divorce in addition to adultery, such as cruel and inhuman treatment, abandonment for two or more years, confinement in a prison for three or more years, and an agreed-upon separation of two years.[28]

In addition, the final bill also contained an elaborate mechanism for counseling spouses who filed for divorce, in the hope of effecting reconciliations. Its sponsors justified the mandatory counseling on the grounds that it would prevent impetuous divorces. The provision was also in keeping with the belief that therapeutic procedures would heal ill marriages. Its real significance, however, was that it soothed the concerns of conservatives in the legislature who remained uncomfortable with liberalizing the divorce law. Although some legislators opposed conciliation because of its cost and because of skepticism about its effectiveness, it remained in the bill because it served as the bond that held together the coalition in favor of divorce reform.

Despite the considerable maneuvering required for the proposal to become law, it attracted little public attention. The final debate in the state senate in April, 1966 was chosen as the first session to be televised, apparently because it would show that legislative body in a good light rather than because it might exhibit a fierce debate on a burning public issue. There is little evidence that the public was particularly aroused by the issue, and newspapers covered the legislative process in only a desultory way. Twenty years after the event, legislators did not remember being deluged by mail as they had been when they considered abortion reform. In 1985 when I interviewed the principals in this legislative effort, one of them asserted that the outcome of the vote had always been a certainty; there simply was no question but that the law would be passed.[29] The fact that divorce was not a burning social issue undoubtedly helped the sponsors of reform in New York. The low-keyed, low-visibility path taken by New York's reform insured that it would arouse little opposition. The Catholic church apparently calculated that it should use its influence on abortion reform (which it had vigorously opposed) and increased financial assistance to its parochial schools (which passed the same session). No other group existed with divorce on its agenda.

Once passed, legislators found it easy to alter the law's original provisions. Within four years, the legislature further eased divorce by reducing the waiting period for a divorce after a separation from two years to one. That change was widely interpreted as the equivalent of no-fault, although New York never abandoned fault grounds of divorce and never explicitly endorsed no-fault divorce. The legislature abolished the concil-iation procedure in 1973 because its expense and ineffective-ness had become burdensome. Moreover, it was no longer needed as a legislative compromise.

The effort to reform divorce laws had mixed consequences for the principals in the effort. Howard Spellman won appoint-ment as director of Manhattan's conciliation bureau but could not save it from the legislature's axe. The senate sponsor of the bill went on to run for a vacant congressional seat but failed to win the election; instead, he turned to a law practice in a prestigious New York City firm. The assembly sponsor of the bill later became a borough president in New York City and went into the media business upon retiring from politics. Al-though all three were perhaps attracted to the issue because of its entrepreneurial potential, the enactment of divorce law re-form did not mark a significant turning point in their careers. On the national scene, New York's accomplishment won little praise. Divorce reformers welcomed New York into the twen-tieth century but did not perceive its new law as innovative. When it was adopted in 1966, no one recognized it as no-fault divorce. Such innovation in divorce law came from elsewhere.

4

California's Bold Step

It remained for California to step into the future and explicitly embrace the no-fault concept in divorce. California illustrates the potential for innovation through a routine policy-making process, for it was the first state to adopt no-fault divorce in the context of a thorough reform of its divorce procedures; yet it did so with minimal controversy.

The Social and Political Context of California's Divorce Reform

No-fault was the sort of innovation that many Americans have come to expect of California. That state has long been viewed as an incubator for novel social ideas. Its population had the reputation of adopting a relaxed life style that included not only suburban living and patio barbecues, but also loose marriages and easy divorces. It was, after all, the home of Hollywood; and while the escapades of movie stars did not typify the average Californian, they established an ambience of nonchalance and experimentation that sometimes permitted Californians to adopt novel ideas.

California in the mid-1960s differed from New York in many ways. California's population had much shallower roots than New York's. The families of most Californians had moved west from elsewhere in the United States since the Great Depression, leaving behind other relatives. They lived in rapidly growing cities which had been ranches and fruit orchards a few years earlier. California's ethnic composition was quite different from that of eastern states because more of its ethnics were Oriental and later Chicano as well as Irish, Italian, and black. Its Catholic population was smaller than New York's, and the church had not acquired as open a political role. Even in the 1960s, ethnicity played a different and smaller role in California politics than in New York; it was more important that ballot tickets be balanced along geographic lines that recognized the gulf between southern and northern California than that Irish or Italian candidates be offset with blacks or Jews.

Fluidity marked California's politics as it characterized its people. It had been possible for Earl Warren to run for governor on both the Republican and Democratic tickets. The legislature was organized along partisan lines, but it was possible for Republicans to support a Democrat for presiding officer of the assembly as late as 1980.[1] Nonpartisanship had become much more entrenched in California than in New York, while machine politics based on patronage scarcely existed. The major political organizations centered on ideological issues in statewide elections and recruited volunteer workers to the California Republican Assembly and the California Democratic Council rather than to "regular" party organizations.

The 1960s were marked by many political crosscurrents in California. In 1958, California elected the liberal (and Catholic) Edmund Brown, Sr. to the governorship and kept him in office until the conservative Ronald Reagan defeated his third-term bid in 1966. Racial tension erupted in the Los Angeles Watts neighborhood riot in 1965 and in Oakland in 1968, together with simultaneous riots in other northern cities, causing the nation to recognize that race relations were not just a southern problem. The "free speech movement" at the University of California's Berkeley campus focused attention on the rebellious hippy style of a conspicuous minority of its youth. A sometimes raucous but always tense campaign to liberalize California's abortion law occupied the attention of many during the last years of the decade. That bill reached Governor Reagan's desk only a few months before no-fault divorce.[2]

The intellectual climate surrounding divorce was also somewhat different in California than in New York. Traditional values of family life rooted in religion dominated discussions in New York. Californians more openly espoused the newer clinical and therapeutic conceptions[3] which saw marital failure as a symptom of psychological incompatibility and maladjustment rather than as an indication of sin. Such ideas had won widespread acceptance among mental health professionals by the 1960s throughout the United States, but in California they were publicly articulated with stark clarity in legislative hearings. Consider this exchange in October, 1964, between the chair of the legislative study committee considering divorce legislation and a psychiatrist who was testifying before the committee:

CHAIRMAN WILLSON: Would you enumerate in the order of their frequency, as causes for divorce, alcoholism, premarital pregnancy, sexual problems, and gambling? Which could you, from your experience, enumerate as being the worst offender and so on?

DR. MILLIGAN: To me all of those are effects; they are all effects of the same thing . . . gross emotional immaturity. . . . Emotional immaturity is a state of decadence or regression that the individual experiences because somehow or another, in this pattern of growth, he was not able to devise better solutions, better emotionality, better emotional solutions to problems.

CHAIRMAN WILLSON: Would that mean then that every divorce is the result of immaturity?

DR. MILLIGAN: I certainly would say that.

CHAIRMAN WILLSON: All right. Now do you think that every person who seeks a divorce is sick? . . .

DR. MILLIGAN: If you mean sick in terms of emotional immaturity to the extent that the individual cannot take care of his ordinary affairs with good judgment and that includes realizing a marriage, being able to stick with the problems and accept them, then I think it is a sickness.[4]

The therapeutic view received unexpected support from the religious sector when in June of 1966, just after New York had passed its new divorce law, a committee appointed by the Archbishop of Canterbury of the Church of England issued its report on divorce. That report, *Putting Asunder*, advocated eliminating adultery and other marital offenses as grounds for divorce and replacing them with marital breakdown. The English commission couched its recommendations in conservative language which would permit judges the discretion to "dissolve the marriage if, and only if, having regard to the interests of society as well as of those immediately affected by its decision, it judged it wrong to maintain the legal existence of a relationship that was beyond all probability of existing again."[5] Moreover, if the court were not convinced that the marriage "had in fact broken down irreparably, [it] would have a duty to refuse a decree despite the express agreement of the parties."[6] However, the commission's view that divorce was justified when marriages had broken down and its support for no-fault divorce were unequivocal. The publication of this church report made advocacy of no-fault appear much less radical than assemblyman Willson asserted. The report arrived just in time to buttress California's no-fault proposal, which itself was published at the end of 1966.[7]

In addition, by the mid-1960s the no-fault concept had gained considerable visibility in other contexts. Workmen's compensation, adopted in the first decades of the twentieth century, explicitly replaced a fault-based system of compensating workers for injuries incurred in industrial accidents.[8] In the 1950s and early 1960s proposals for adopting a no-fault automobile accident insurance plan had evoked considerable discussion and controversy. Those plans, eventually adopted in many states, were intended to eliminate fault-based litigation and replace it with compensation of insured drivers from their own insurance policies. No personal connection existed between advocates of no-fault automobile insurance and no-fault divorce,[9] but discussions of no-fault accident insurance familiarized people with the concept and made it appear less radical when it was proposed for divorce.

One further distinction differentiated California from New York. California's divorce law was in practice among the most lenient in the nation. As Herma Hill Kay, a teacher of family law at the University of California's Boalt Hall School of Law and a leader in the reform movement, put it: "It was impossible to make divorce easier in California than it already was."[10] It was, however, a fault-grounded divorce law. To obtain a divorce, husband or wife had to demonstrate that the other spouse had committed a marital offense, such as adultery, cruelty, or desertion.[11] In most cases, the wife was the plaintiff and her complaint usually alleged cruelty, which encompassed a host of sins ranging from disparaging remarks to spouse abuse. The testimony was often arranged and fake, disguising a mutual or negotiated decision to end the marriage. It was this element of dishonesty that provoked some of the proponents of change to seek a no-fault statute and, as in New York, it provided a technical cover for advocating a revolutionary liberalization. But unlike New York, the production of fraudulent evidence was not a visible industry, and the no-fault concept was openly discussed in California, having even been articulated in a California Supreme Court case as early as 1952 in an opinion by the renowned Chief Justice Roger Traynor.[12]

A high divorce rate paralleled California's easy divorce law. Although California's divorce rate did not approach Nevada's and was indeed only eleventh in the nation, it was perceived as being a divorce-prone state by its natives. However, California's law had one quirk that motivated some people to migrate to Nevada for their divorce: a California divorce was not final until one year had passed. During this interlocutory period, ex-spouses were not permitted to remarry. This provision had been intended to prevent hasty divorces motivated by a passing fancy for another man or woman. In fact, it proved to be a major inconvenience, because in the 1960s extramarital cohabitation had not yet become widespread or socially accepted, but many people getting a divorce wanted to begin a new family soon after ending their first marriage.

Thus, on the eve of the effort to change California's divorce law, there was nothing as drastic as New York's antiquated law to motivate change, although the state was in a good position to experiment with something as bold as no-fault. No-fault fit the therapeutic and clinical view of marriage and divorce that had gained professional currency. It had antecedents in other legal arenas such as no-fault automobile accident insurance and workmen's compensation. And it had the sanction of such a seemingly conservative body as the Church of England.

Innovation through Routine Policy Making

Innovation is usually thought to involve at least two stages. The first is the identification of a problem that involves a serious performance gap requiring a solution.[13] The second is the formulation of a solution. Thereafter, those responsible for making policy decisions must be convinced that the solution is a viable and attractive response to the problem.

Performance gaps are usually a prerequisite for innovation because people are loath to change adequately working procedures.[14] The character of such gaps, however, varies considerably because they are subjective phenomena. It is rare for everyone to agree that a policy is failing or to concur on the dimensions of the failure. Often the client or objects of a policy have a different perception than its administrators, as when people who must wait for months to receive a government payment complain but the administrators of the agency making the payment think all is proceeding normally. The measurement instrument is frequently at issue, with one group arguing that it indicates failure while another points to a different set of facts which suggests adequate performance from their perspective. Thus, parents may complain that their children are not learning to read well enough while school administrators point with satisfaction to rising test score levels. Even the goals of a policy may become subject to dispute, as when one group of citizens calls on the police to stop speeding drivers on their residential street while another group decries the waste of police on traffic enforcement while drug sales flourish.

Performance gaps may be the result of a gradual decay in the operation of a policy or the consequence of a sudden external shock which dramatically changes the conditions confronting administrators. In the former case, a series of small events pulls a policy's achievements increasingly away from its stated goals, creating a gradual awareness of the policy's inadequacy. The social security crisis of the late 1970s was an example of such a gradual decay, when slowly rising payments were not matched by rising revenues for the system. At other times, performance gaps occur because of a sudden change in the environment which the policy and its administrators cannot accommodate. The discovery of AIDS, for instance, suddenly created a public health crisis which pointed to the inadequacy of existing measures for the prevention of sexually transmitted diseases.

In every case the definition of the performance gap is both subjective and of central importance to the subsequent adoption of innovative solutions. Because it is subjective, it may be manipulated by those seeking to promote or block a change. Both sides, however, recognize its crucial significance for the adoption process, because the manner in which the gap is defined either excites or lulls potential opponents. Defined expansively, a performance gap invites wide group participation and public controversy; defined narrowly, it demarcates a restricted field of groups and makes it unlikely that the media will publicize the push for reform.

The formulation of solutions is often dominated by self-appointed experts. The solutions may be specifically designed to address the performance gap, or they may have been devised for other purposes and simply found available for application to the newly discovered performance gap. In the former case, decision makers embark on a rational search-and-choice process in which experts examine the dimensions of the problem, consider available alternative solutions in terms of their promised costs and benefits, and recommend the one with the greatest potential net benefits. Since many of the costs and benefits are difficult to measure, the process depends much more on informed intuition than on mechanical calculation; consequently, the conclusions drawn by the experts are often subject to conflicting interpretations. In many instances, however, the selection of an innovation may be quite different and involve less rational choice and more coincidence. As March and Olsen suggest,[15] solutions are sometimes devised for other purposes and looking for problems to which they may be attached. A common example is the personal computer which a businessman may purchase for status reasons and then leave to sit on his desk; he may ultimately use it to make corporate financial calculations for which he had never previously felt a need. In this instance, the computer created both the performance gap and its solution. It is likely that experts identify such a solution because of their familiarity with new ideas. Its adoption, however, very much depends on the constellation of participants who happen to be present when the decision is made. Thus, the innovation process may involve much less rational calculation than the search-and-choose model suggests.

The adoption of no-fault divorce in California illustrates these processes in the context of routine policy making. It shows how a major alteration of public policy may occur with few of the trappings of public debate and controversy. It involved the manipulation of the definition of a performance gap and the adoption of an innovative solution which was waiting to be matched to the problem of divorce.

The Reformers

A key to the distinctive development of divorce reform in California was the identity of the reformers and the manner in which they defined the performance gap and devised their no-fault solution. As other students of innovation have found, the impetus for reform came from a small band of self-appointed experts who elevated the discrepancies between black-letter law and the law-in-action to the status of a performance gap and formulated the solution.

The experts consisted of a small group of elite matrimonial lawyers in the San Francisco Bay area who had long regretted the bitterness engendered by the adversarial divorce process which they witnessed in their professional lives. They felt that much of the conflict they saw in their offices and in divorce courtrooms was the unnecessary product of statutes which required the fabrication of ugly events that would justify divorce on the grounds of extreme cruelty. Their goal was both to eliminate the perjurious evidence which tainted matrimonial lawyers in the eyes of their colleagues and to humanize the divorce process by decreasing the level of conflict. They had quietly worked for many years to win the support of mental health professionals and the organized bar for such a reform.

It is worth noting that some plausible goals which would have sparked intense opposition were not embraced by the reformers. They did not explicitly advocate making divorce easier because divorce was better than family conflict. They did not formulate their goals in terms of achieving equality for women,[16] nor did they champion divorce reform in order to permit greater individual choice among alternative family forms. Instead, the reformers hewed to objectives which appeared politically innocuous.

At the group's core were Herma Hill Kay, a law professor at Boalt Hall (University of California, Berkeley), Richard Dinkelspiel, a San Francisco attorney who was also prominent in Catholic lay circles, Kathryn Gehrels, a prominent San Francisco attorney who handled many upper-class divorces, and Irving Phillips, a psychiatrist associated with the University of California Medical School. These four, who enjoyed both professional and friendship bonds, were interested in no-fault reform principally because it appealed to them on intellectual grounds. They saw it as a cure for the hypocrisy which permeated divorce proceedings in California as they had in New York, and they saw such a change as worthy of the long tradition of reform leadership which characterized much California law making.

A second group of divorce reformers centered around Los Angeles and consisted of Pearce Young, a prominent assemblyman, Roger Pfaff a vocal judge who presided over the conciliation court in Los Angeles, and several Beverly Hills matrimonial lawyers. The Los Angeles contingent did not always agree with the San Francisco Bay area proponents of divorce law reform, but they provided the necessary southern leg of interest in divorce reform so that the effort could not be dismissed as a northern California aberration.

Laying the Foundation for Reform

As early as 1962, the legislature's Assembly Interim Committee on the Judiciary[17] considered amending the state's domestic relations law, but that committee concerned itself principally with changing the law's provisions for an interlocutory divorce that forced people to wait a year before remarrying. It never reached more fundamental issues. Two years later, domestic relations law was again targeted by the assembly's interim judiciary committee.[18] That committee conducted a wide-ranging examination of California's marriage and divorce laws. It held hearings from January to October of 1964 in Santa Monica, Sacramento, and twice in Los Angeles. It heard numerous witnesses who ascribed divorce to a variety of causes ranging from the advent of the automobile (where out-of-wedlock pregnancies were conceived in back seats) to the changing role of women; they discussed problems of property distribution and child custody. Among the remedies mentioned were family life education courses in schools, marriage counseling, a family court, mandatory divorce counseling, and gender-neutral provisions for child custody.

Many of the members of the core group of divorce reformers testified. Herma Hill Kay addressed each of the four hearings; Judge Pfaff also appeared at each. Los Angeles attorneys Harry Fain and Stuart Walzer, later members of the governor's commission, presented their views, as did the later executive director of the governor's commission, Aiden Gough. Assemblyman Pearce Young, later co-chair of the governor's commission, also participated in the committee's work.

These hearings provided an opportunity for Kay and others to introduce the no-fault concept and some of the other innovations which later marked the 1969 law. No-fault surfaced at the very beginning, when at the committee's January, 1964 hearing Kay testified:

. . . as long as we are not going to require any detailed evidence as to the grounds for divorce and as long as we have a large number of default divorces in this State, it seems to me a good idea to permit parties to have at least one ground for divorce in which fault is not made necessary.[19]

By October, Kay was ready to make much more specific and far-reaching proposals. She pointed to a Pennsylvania legislative proposal drafted by New York's divorce expert Henry H. Foster, Jr., which unabashedly favored divorce by mutual consent "which of course is true as a matter of practice now but it is not the way the statutes are drafted."[20] However, not all members of the committee were ready to support her proposal. The chairman on that day, assemblyman Willson, demurred saying: "I recognize the problem that you would have in trying to get such a ground through the Legislature and through the people of the state. . ."[21] When Kay became more explicit in her support for no-fault, Willson interrupted: "Well now, Professor Kay, I can't subscribe to that. You will have to exclude me from that. I think it is possible for a woman to be wrong or a man to be wrong and break up a marriage."[22] That did not deter Kay from proceeding to advocate elimination of adversarial-style proceedings in divorce cases and establishment of a new family court system to hear all matters related to divorce and other family problems. Thus, two years before the Archbishop of Canterbury's report made no-fault a widely discussed concept and before New York's divorce reform law, Kay outlined the basic features of a complete reform of American divorce law.

Kay was not the only witness to make wide-ranging proposals, although she was probably the most widely respected witness to do so. Judge Pfaff urged extension of his conciliation procedures to the entire state so that more marriages would be saved. Representatives of the U.S. Divorce Reform League advocated taking divorce cases out of court and giving men more rights with respect to their children.

The committee's report, however, scarcely reflected such proposals. It made few specific recommendations and lamely suggested the need for further study and deliberation. No immediate action came from the year's work.

Formulation of the Divorce Proposals

After a hiatus of sixteen months, divorce reforms suddenly revived. Governor Edmund Brown appointed a commission on the family in May of 1966, just as he was preparing to run for a third term against the movie actor and political novice, Ronald Reagan. The idea for the commission seems to have come from the Bay area group, which had a conduit to the governor's office through a former law student of Kay.[23] The official proclamation of the commission did not reveal its likely outcome; its title was the innocuous "Governor's Commission on the Family." It was charged to "study and suggest revision, where necessary, of the substantive laws of California relating to the family," to examine the feasibility of developing courses in family life for California's schools, to consider the possibility of developing a uniform national standard for marriage and divorce jurisdiction, and to look into the establishment of a system of family courts.[24] In fact, the commission responded only to the first and last elements of this charge.

The commission included many of the core Bay area persons who had pressed for divorce law reform, as well as some key legislators and prominent jurists and lawyers from the Los Angeles area. The spark plugs of the commission, however, were the Bay area members, who formulated many of its recommendations. Potential opposition from some conservative members was averted by the illness of one their key spokesmen, Judge Pfaff, who urged conciliation procedures but resisted more fundamental changes; his dissent was limited to a letter to Dinkelspiel, who was co-chair, but it was not printed in the commission's report.[25]

Unlike the interim commission of the legislature, the governor's commission held no public hearings. Indeed, it seems to have worked entirely in the shadow of the heated gubernatorial campaign that took place during most of its life. It issued no press releases and its work did not reach the attention of the media until it was completed and its report published. Under this cloak of obscurity, the commission forged its radical proposal; but while the commission worked, Governor Brown lost the gubernatorial election. With the much more conservative Ronald Reagan in the wings, the commission rushed to complete its work before inaugural day; it managed to convey its report to Governor Brown just two weeks before he left office and its authority expired.

The governor's commission was careful to veil its proposals in as conservative a guise as possible. It first highlighted its plan to consolidate all family disputes in a newly constituted family court that would be available in every county. That court and the conciliation and counseling services connected with it were to help save families from stress and dissolution. Moreover, the commission clothed its report in pro-family vocabulary. It argued that the goal of the law should be "to further the stability of the family"[26] and that the existing law

represents by its ineptitude an abdication of the public interest in, and responsibility toward, the family as the basic unit of our society. The direction of the law must be, as we have said, toward family stability—toward preventing divorce where it is not warranted, and toward reducing its harmful effects where it is necessary.[27]

The commission's second thrust was its radical contribution, but it too was described with a conservative vocabulary. Claiming that it simply wished to align the law with the divorce process as it really worked, the commission proposed eliminating all fault grounds for divorce and replacing them with the requirement that irreparable breakdown of the marriage exist. Lest that this be seen as an invitation to easy divorce, the commission wrote:

We cannot overemphasize that this standard does not permit divorce by consent, wherein marriage is treated as wholly a private contract terminable at the pleasure of the parties without any effective intervention by society. The standard we propose requires the community to assert its interest in the status of the family, and permits dissolution of the marriage only after it has been subjected to a penetrating scrutiny and the judicial process has provided the parties with all of the resources of social science in aid of conciliation.[28]

Note that the commission invoked not only society's interest in stable families but also the therapeutic potential of science that might be harnessed by its proposal. In addition, the commission quoted at length from the Archbishop of Canterbury's report in support of its no-fault proposal.[29]

In order to reduce the law's contribution to marital conflict, the commission also suggested abandoning the conventional vocabulary of litigation in divorce cases. Instead of styling divorce actions in the usual way, "Jones v. Jones," cases were to be referred to as "In re. the marriage of Jones." Instead of a complaint, a "petition of inquiry" was to initiate the proceedings. Even the term "divorce" was to be replaced with "marital dissolution." Each of these proposals closely followed the suggestions made by Herma Hill Kay two years earlier to the interim study committee of the California legislature. Kay, of course, was a key member of the governor's commission and played a central role in drafting its recommendations.

A third set of proposals concerned the disposition of property at divorce. The existing rules permitted property division to be governed by fault. California was already a community property state in which both spouses had a claim to any property accumulated during their marriage. However, innocent parties in a divorce case were eligible for more than half of the community property. When the commission proposed banishing fault, a new rule had to be devised. Without much discussion of its potential consequences, the commission recommended establishing a presumption of equal distribution of community property, except in circumstances when some other division seemed appropriate.[30] Alimony also was redefined. It too was set loose from a consideration of fault and was instead based on need "for such a period of time as the court may deem just and reasonable."[31]

Finally, some questions of child custody were addressed. The commission took note of the fact that many mothers no longer provided full-time care even for very young children, but rather entrusted them to day care and pre-school nurseries. Consequently, the commission recommended ending the practice of automatically favoring mothers in deciding custody and establishing a new standard which required that the court consider the "best interests of the child" in determining which parent (or other person) should have custody of children of broken marriages. The report, however, gave little consideration to the precise meaning of that standard.[32]

Despite the commission's elite membership and radical suggestions, its report produced scarcely a ripple of reaction. It was released in mid-December of 1966, during the last days of the Brown administration, as political reporters were speculating on the intentions of the incoming Reagan team and as the rest of world prepared for the Christmas holidays. Because the commission had operated without any publicity, few persons even knew that such recommendations had been made.

Backstage Negotiations and Legislative Maneuvering

Obscurity probably helped more than hurt the prospects of the commission's recommendations, because it shielded them from potential opponents. At the same time, it reflected the absence of organized opposition to its suggestions, because no lobbyist in Sacramento sounded an alarm.

The lack of hostility from the Catholic church was particularly notable. The Commission's report had tip-toed around the potential conflict between civil divorce and religious norms of family life. The report included a discussion of the matter in the following words:

Our study has convinced us that . . . a "breakdown-of-marriage" standard in no way derogates ecclesiastical doctrines of the indissolubility of marriage. When a Civil Court orders the dissolution of a marriage, it does not reach the canonical bonds of the union; it acts rather on the complex of legal rights and duties that make up the legal status of marriage.[33]

However, the commission did not simply rely on this argument. The absence of Catholic opposition was the result of careful cultivation of the Catholic hierarchy. That was facilitated by staffing decisions which substantially assisted communication with the northern California hierarchy. At the outset Governor Brown shrewdly appointed Richard Dinkelspiel as co-chair of the commission. Dinkelspiel was not only one of the core members of the Bay Area reform group, but more importantly, he was a very prominent Catholic layman with ties to the hierarchy. In addition, he was well known and widely respected in the San Francisco and California bars. Secondly, the governor appointed Aidan Gough to be the commission's executive director. Gough was a young law professor at Santa Clara University and perhaps the most available expert in matrimonial law. But he taught in a Jesuit institution, his university's president (who had encouraged him to take the position) was the brother of the Bishop of Stockton, and his family was friendly with the Archbishop of San Francisco.[34] Those ties were helpful in keeping the bishops of northern California informed about the commission's work. The commission won their timely backing for its proposals in the form of a public statement of support for the commission's recommendations before Cardinal McIntyre of Los Angeles, who had more conservative leanings, discovered the outcome of the commission's work. Given the open support of the northern bishops, it was difficult for McIntyre to oppose them publicly, whatever his private thoughts.

Obscurity also permitted quiet cultivation of support for the commission's recommendations. California did not lack political controversies to occupy the attention of its legislature. Governor Reagan sought to reduce state expenditures; the campaign for abortion reform was nearing its climax; the state, like the remainder of the nation, was riveted on Vietnam and the growing domestic opposition to that war. During these distractions, proponents sought endorsement from the California

Bar Association. Although the bar proposed numerous changes to the commission's proposal, it accepted its main thrust and told its lobbyist to support a bill which incorporated the bar's suggestions and the commission's proposals.[35] Further, although the commission's proposals were introduced into the legislature in 1967, they lay fallow for two years. This interlude was used to familiarize legislators with the revolutionary concepts of the bill.[36] When the legislature finally turned its attention to the bill, it seemed less radical and had garnered substantial support.

In addition, the political landscape of California changed. The Democrats had not only lost the governor's office but also their comfortable margin in the legislature; in the next election in 1968 they became the minority. Pearce Young left the legislature for a judgeship in 1966; another legislative supporter, Willie Shoemaker, lost his seat in 1968. Moreover, the new governor made clear his opposition to new social expenditures, and the family court proposal surely would be expensive. Thus some revision of the commission's proposal seemed inevitable.

By 1969, supporters of no-fault felt that with concerted effort they might win passage of the bills. The principal sponsor was of one of the commission's members, a Republican state senator, Donald Grunsky, who had not been especially active in the commission's work but who was deeply committed to its product. He brought to the task his credentials as a prominent conservative and his position as chair of the Senate Judiciary Committee. Grunsky's major problems in obtaining passage of the bill were allaying the opposition of incumbent judges to the establishment of a new family court system (which might also prove quite expensive) and winning the cooperation of the chair of the assembly judiciary committee, Los Angeles assemblyman James Hayes, who had not previously participated in the development of the proposals but presented his own bill as an alternative. The result was that some of the commission's proposals were dropped. Judicial opposition as well as the cost problem was met by abandoning the family court proposal which lay at the heart of much of what the commission sought to accomplish. Grunsky avoided the potential opposition of the Los Angeles assemblyman by graciously stepping aside and allowing him to assume the role of principal spokesperson for the reform,[37] but that meant several other changes for the commission's plan.[38] One was an attempt to define what "irreconcilable differences" meant by referring to "grounds" supporting dissolution of the marriage; that language appeared to reintroduce fault, although later practice proved that fear unfounded. Another alteration was the bill's failure to mention the possibility of unequal distribution of property when economic circumstances warranted it. The bill also seemed to endorse transitional maintenance in place of permanent alimony by telling judges to consider the spouse's ability to earn a living in determining the amount of alimony. Finally, Grunsky and the supporters of no-fault had to accept the addition of one traditional ground for divorce, mental illness. That did not change the legislation substantively, but the Los Angeles assemblyman insisted upon it.

By the time these negotiations took place, supporters of no-fault had quietly generated public support in the form of newspaper editorials and constituent letters. Even Catholic groups wrote to legislators in support of the no-fault bill.[39] Thus, legislators like the Los Angeles assemblyman found divorce reform an attractive issue upon which to build their legislative reputations, even when their general policy stance was a conservative one.[40] In the meantime, the liberals who had drafted the commission's proposals remained discretely in the background. The coalition built by Grunsky led to legislative approval by June of 1969 with less public maneuvering and attention than had accompanied New York's much more modest legislation three years earlier.

Governor Reagan, himself once divorced, proved no obstacle to the bill and signed it into law with only a mild plea for future fine-tuning. It became effective in 1970 and came to be known as the nation's first no-fault divorce law.

The new law followed the general thrust of the governor's commission with respect to the grounds for divorce. It eliminated all fault grounds and permitted divorce only upon a showing of incurable insanity or "irreconcilable differences which have caused the irremediable breakdown of the marriage."[41] The statute mandated the new style of divorce petitions which avoided the terminology of conventional litigation. It eliminated all consideration of fault with respect to property division. However, it went further than the governor's commission in mandating equal division of property by omitting the commission's recommendation by narrowing the exceptional circumstances justifying an unequal division.[42] Finally, the new law altered alimony so that it would ordinarily be temporary support for the dependent spouse while he or she became self-sufficient.[43]

The official legislative history of the law claimed that the new law was intended to facilitate gender equality. Kay argues that this was an entirely erroneous assertion.[44] Indeed, the new law was not in any way a feminist product. The alimony provisions as enacted were less favorable to women than those that had been recommended by the commission. The principal change was that the legislature added the provision that the "ability of the supported spouse to engage in gainful employment" be considered in alimony decisions, thereby converting alimony to a transitional payment while the dependent spouse entered the labor market. In addition, the new law did not include the commission's recommendation to end the presumption in favor of mothers of young children in deciding custody. Instead, it reenacted the tender years doctrine.[45] Finally, the new law reenacted several provisions which were soon to become anathema to feminists. One section stated: "The husband is the head of the family. He may choose any reasonable place or mode of living, and the wife must conform thereto."[46] Another confirmed the husband's right to manage community property during the marriage.[47] Gender equality was neither sought nor achieved by California's no-fault law. Indeed, there is no evidence that feminists were active supporters of the new law or held any expectation that women would be treated better under the new law than the old.[48]

Conclusion

California's proponents of no-fault divorce skillfully maneuvered to utilize the routine policy process and to avoid the conflictual. They defined the performance gap in divorce laws narrowly and restricted interest group involvement. Adroit maneuvering sidestepped potential opposition from the Catholic church. Feminists were scarcely engaged because they apparently did not perceive the revolutionary character of the law, since it had been presented (like New York's) as a largely technical revision that simply brought statutory law into conformity with actual practice.

The advocates of divorce reform commanded considerable expertise and worked hard to keep the issue in their hands through the formation of the governor's commission. They emphasized the compatibility of their proposals with existing legal practice even though their suggestions clashed with black-letter law. They sought to enhance the legitimacy of their proposals by making copious references to the recommendations of the Archbishop of Canterbury's report.

While the California no-fault statute was the product of many years of deliberation, the deliberative process attracted very little public attention. None of the principals claimed fame or fortune as the result of the law's enactment. While the leaders of the abortion struggle climbed to more prominent national office,[49] the proponents of no-fault remained in relative obscurity. Perhaps the most telling evidence of the invisibility of the revision process is the complete absence of its mention in the oral history of the Brown and Reagan administrations. Interviews exist for activists over abortion proposals and many other legal initiatives, but none for those involved in the no-fault law.

However, the proponents of divorce reform almost made a fatal error. Carried by their enthusiasm for the therapeutic model, they advocated establishing a new tier of courts to handle family matters and facilitate conciliation. The expense of that proposal and its challenge to the authority of sitting judges threatened to arouse strong opposition. Those elements of the proposal were, however, dropped during its legislative consideration. Without that concession, it is likely that the issue of divorce reform would have become much more conflictual and would have faced Governor Reagan's fiscal veto. By eliminating the costly elements of their recommendations, no-fault advocates were able to utilize the routine policy process to achieve divorce reform.

5

Nationalizing No-Fault Divorce: The NCCUSL

Policy making involves not only public but also private arenas. That is particularly true of policy changes which are defined as technical legal matters where specialized groups of legal experts play an exceptionally important role. Two such arenas exist in the United States. One is the American Law Institute, which periodically issues "Restatements of the Law of . . ." particular areas of the law, such as torts, that become influential accounts of black letter law in the United States. It was this group that issued the "Restatement of the Law of Torts" in 1965 articulating a rule of strict liability which came to play a prominent role in the litigation over asbestos damages.[1] The second is the National Conference of Commissioners on Uniform State Laws (NCCUSL), which issues uniform state laws to guide state legislatures. The NCCUSL joined the American Law Institute in drafting the Uniform Commercial Code, a widely adopted body of commercial law in the United States. The NCCUSL was also a key actor in recommending no-fault divorce to the states.

The same process of routine policy making occurred in the NCCUSL as in California. The manner in which the divorce reformers in the NCCUSL managed to keep no-fault in the routine policy-making mode goes far in explaining how they succeeded in developing a uniform marriage and divorce act despite the organization's long record of failure in divorce law reform.

The NCCUSL is a unique quasi-public body. It was organized in 1892 to promote, among other reforms, a uniform marriage and divorce act for the states. However, after several unsuccessful attempts it abandoned that task and turned to the development of other uniform state laws on such subjects as wills, securities, and the determination of death.[2] It is composed entirely of legal experts. State governors appoint its members from the ranks of law professors, prestigious attorneys, and well-placed legislators. Its budget comes from state appropriations as well as from such grants as it can procure. It works through drafting committees whose products are then debated at its annual conference and usually adopted with only minor changes. Its proposals then go to the American Bar Association (ABA), which generally endorses them. The double endorsement of the NCCUSL and ABA establishes the so-called "uniform act" as an influential model for state legislatures. Few uniform acts win approval from state legislatures without substantial alteration to suit local conditions, but the fundamental concepts underlying those model laws are given a powerful thrust by the endorsement of the NCCUSL and ABA.

However, unlike state legislatures, the NCCUSL avoids the limelight of publicity and the media seldom report its activities. It does not hold public hearings and is not subject to overt pressure group or partisan politics as are legislatures. Its committees often consult with representatives of diverse groups in order to increase the likelihood that its model statutes will win the approval of state legislatures, but such consultation occurs in a relatively unsystematic way through private rather than public channels. All of these characteristics made the NCCUSL an ideal vehicle for promoting no-fault divorce.

Unlike a legislature such as California's, the NCCUSL operates in the broad national arena rather than in the narrow confines of a single state and must reflect national conditions. It usually is more conservative than venturesome California, a fact that makes its adoption of no-fault particularly significant, for by its endorsement of this new standard, the conference placed the cachet of respectability upon no-fault. But it did not happen without considerable effort.

The National Environment for No-Fault Divorce

The Intellectual Environment

As we have already indicated, no-fault was an idea that was increasingly in vogue in several areas of the law. It had been most prominently discussed with respect to auto accident insurance, where reformers proposed that instead of attempting to assess blame for auto accidents, insurance companies should insure their own drivers, who would be reimbursed for damages and injuries regardless of who was at fault. The most conspicuous statement of that idea was published in the mid-1960s by two law professors, Robert E. Keeton and Jeffrey O'Connell, who were its principal architects.[3] The Keeton-O'Connell no-fault plan was an attractive idea in the personal injury field because in many accidents fault was shared by several drivers, while in others no one was obviously at fault; thus, ascertaining fault was often an exercise in futility and fictionalization. Moreover, reformers hoped that the implementation of this idea would reduce the number of trials and the amount of time it took for people to be reimbursed for their claims.

Divorce had several parallels to traffic accidents. Like those mishaps, it was often difficult to assess blame in failed marriages. While a single event often precipitated the breakup, hundreds of trivial disputes generally preceded it. Like personal injury suits, divorce cases often took long to conclude and the few which went to trial consumed much court time.

However, the link between no-fault in auto accident cases and divorce law remained a conceptual one; its advocacy in one field did not directly affect the other. The principal proponent of no-fault auto accident insurance had no interest in the divorce field and does not remember any overlap between his promotion of the no-fault idea for personal injury suits and its emergence in family law.[4] Likewise, the champions of no-fault divorce had played no role in its promotion in the auto accident field.[5] Moreover, whereas the application of no-fault to auto accident cases was hotly disputed by personal injury plaintiff lawyers, in part because it threatened to reduce their caseload by diverting claims to a purely administrative procedure, divorce lawyers were generally not hostile to no-fault because, among other reasons, divorces would still require court action and considerable litigation. Nevertheless, the no-fault standard for making legal decisions was a much-discussed idea in the 1960s.

It was also familiar to legal scholars acquainted with the law as it had already been adopted in a few East European countries. One of the most eminent family law specialists, University of Chicago law professor Max Rheinstein, disseminated information about those laws in the United States in a series of articles that were widely read by specialists.[6] Moreover, as we have noted, in the mid-1960s no-fault divorce began to be widely discussed in England with the formation of the Archbishop of Canterbury's commission and its report.

Furthermore, the no-fault idea fit well with the therapeutic conceptions of divorce that had become widespread by the 1950s and 1960s. Family breakdown was seen less frequently as sinful and more often as evidence of social maladjustment that could be remedied through therapy. Some marriages could be saved through counseling; in other cases, men and women could be helped to start new marriages by permitting them to escape relationships that had become hopelessly entangled. Assessing blame, as traditional law required, interfered with this process.[7] However, most of these ideas remained confined to a narrow elite of attorneys and therapists and were not widely diffused in the general legal literature on divorce[8] before the 1970s, as witnessed by the fact that no-fault was scarcely mentioned in law review articles on divorce in the early 1960s.[9]

The Social and Political Context

As we have already indicated, divorce became increasingly common in the 1960s. Ordinary people began to notice that their neighbors, friends, and relatives were getting divorces, and the public careers of figures like governors Rockefeller and Reagan survived divorce. Making divorce less adversarial, therefore, was consonant with the increasingly accepted perception that divorce should not be made immensely difficult.

That perception also contributed to keeping divorce reform out of the political limelight. Maintaining the old legal order was not perceived to be an attractive issue among political entrepreneurs. Moreover, the feminist movement—which was reviving just when advocates of no-fault pressed their cause—was distracted by other matters. The dominant feminist organization, the National Organization of Women, was just being organized in 1966; it, and its predecessors, concentrated mostly on advocacy of legalized abortion, on equal legal rights for women, and on issues of direct economic significance to women, such as discrimination at the workplace. The potential consequences of no-fault divorce were scarcely visible to feminists, and they neither supported nor opposed them in their major public statements. The absence of feminist concern also kept anti-feminists away from the divorce issue. Anti-feminists mostly reacted to the agenda of the feminists: feminist advocacy of ERA provoked anti-ERA activity; feminist promotion of abortion aroused anti-abortion agitation. The lack of feminist support, therefore, also helps account for the absence of anti-feminist opposition and of political interest in the issue.

Formulating the Problem

As in California, a key element in channeling divorce reform into the routine policy-making mode was the formulation of the problem in such a manner that it would remain in the domain of technocrats rather than politicos. This was done in much the same manner as in California. A handful of little-known legal experts controlled the formulation of the problem.

The advocates of no-fault divorce were several unconnected groups of practicing lawyers and legal technocrats. Most prominent among the practicing lawyers were two matrimonial attorneys in Newark, New Jersey, Leonard Brown and Bernard Hellring, who had become disenchanted with the fault system of procuring divorces for their clients. They were members of the NCCUSL and thus represented the upper crust of the practicing bar, but they were unknown outside a small circle of elite divorce lawyers. As early as 1966, they prepared a report to the NCCUSL urging the formulation of a committee to draft a new divorce law; they did not use the term no-fault but spoke about it in terms of eliminating cumbersome and misleading "forms of action."[10] They were joined eventually by three law professors who had few prior ties with one another or with the two practicing attorneys. One was NYU's Professor Henry H. Foster, who had built a wide reputation as one of the handful of leading matrimonial law specialists in the United States. Foster was well connected with the New York politicians who had produced the new divorce law in that state, was prominent in the ABA Family Law Section, and knew some of the leaders of the conference. The second law professor was Robert J. Levy of the University of Minnesota, a family law expert who was gaining a reputation for his knowledge of the social science literature on the family, but who had not established a wide reputation outside the scholarly world. The third law professor was Herma Hill Kay, who was a key player in the California reform but who did not know well any of the other core advocates of no-fault. All five were technocrats with no more than weak political affiliations. Moreover, until the conference mobilized to draft a new divorce law, they worked independently; indeed, Levy and Kay, who eventually played key roles in the formulation of the new law, were explicitly recruited into the effort by the conference.

The advocates perceived the problem which required a new divorce law in ways very similar to the California reformers. The problem, as they perceived it, was widespread dissatisfaction with divorce procedures that had become prevalent far beyond New York's and California's boundaries.[11] The complaints had three common themes. First, attorneys throughout the country resented the extensive manufacturing or doctoring of evidence to fit the narrow provisions of existing divorce law. Divorce lawyers were under considerable pressure everywhere to put an acceptable gloss to the domestic discord that accompanied divorce petitions. In most states, the easiest way to do that was to base the divorce action on the mental cruelty provisions of the divorce law, which led attorneys to suggest to clients that they testify that their spouse had been disparaging and that they suffered many sleepless nights as a consequence; alternatively, a fictitious slap to the face evidenced physical cruelty. In truth, adultery may have been a cause for the divorce in some of these cases, while in others there was nothing more than a desire to end the marriage. Another cause for the manufacture of supporting evidence lay in state laws which did not allow as quick a divorce as the client demanded; in response, attorneys arranged phoney out-of-state residences so that the more lenient laws of another state could be used. These practices were no secret. Judges in every state quietly accommodated divorce lawyers by not probing into the truthfulness of the evidence they offered; the judiciary of those states with short residence periods like Nevada's openly participated in what became a substantial trade in divorce, which supported a sizeable segment of the state's economy. Thus, perjury became a silent partner of divorce proceedings and cast a pall on the practice of family law.

The second widespread cause for dissatisfaction with divorce law was that it forced family disputes into the adversarial mode of court actions. Most divorce cases already had an uncomfortably high degree of emotional conflict. Many divorce attorneys felt that the requirements of the adversarial system heightened that conflict to unacceptable levels. Legal norms had several consequences. Clients could not share a common attorney but each had to have his and her own. Attorneys were bound by the ethical standards of the profession to seek the best settlement for their clients rather than a common compromise. The interests of children were poorly represented unless they too had a separate attorney. The system seemed designed to promote and exacerbate conflict, rather than to provide a way to find compromises and to get the divorce in as painless a fashion as possible.

A third common complaint about the nation's divorce laws was that they were a patchwork of provisions that differed for each state. This particularly bothered matrimonial lawyers handling high-status clients who had large property interests at stake and were more likely than others to live in different jurisdictions. Divorces in such cases seemed unnecessarily complicated. Moreover, the differences in divorce laws allowed fathers to escape their custody or support obligations by moving to another state; in some metropolitan areas (like New York City) it involved little more than moving to a different suburb. Consequently, elite divorce lawyers advocated making divorce law uniform throughout the country.

This definition of the problem emphasized the legalistic concerns of the divorce lawyers and usually eschewed larger social issues. For instance, it avoided discussion of the effect of changing divorce rules on the roles of men and women. It implicitly denied any consequences of change for ongoing marriages by presuming that the proposed changes did little more than ratify existing but not legally sanctioned practices. It did not consider the possibility of reforming divorce rules as part of a more far-reaching alteration of family policy in the United States, such as establishing family allowances (which might alter child support obligations) or the institutionalization of child care (which together with a parental leave policy might alter the distribution of child care responsibilities). Instead, the advocates of no-fault divorce framed their proposal in more limited, technical terms and thereby discouraged broader participation in the deliberations over the reforms.

Formulating and Adopting the No-Fault Solution

The NCCUSL's embrace of no-fault divorce occurred in even greater obscurity and under more control of experts than had been the case in California. Motivated by their own disenchantment with divorce laws, Hellring and Brown rekindled the conference's interest in divorce reform in the early 1960s. Focusing their considerable energies on mobilizing the NCCUSL, they succeeded in placing marriage and divorce on its agenda in the mid-1960s.

The first step was to procure funds for the conference to undertake a special study of divorce laws. Hellring and Brown convinced the conference's executive director, Allison Dunham, to search for outside funding. After some unsuccessful exploratory talks with several private foundations, Dunham learned that the Ford Foundation might be receptive to such a proposal, whereupon he secured the assistance of Robert Levy to write a grant application in November, 1965;[12] it yielded a $60,000 grant from Ford in early 1967. Additional funds came from a small grant from the U.S. Department of Health, Education, and Welfare.[13]

With money in hand, the conference appointed a new committee to study the matter and draft a uniform law. However, Hellring and Brown had annoyed the leadership of the conference with their persistent badgering for quick action and were dropped as co-chairs of the committee and only reluctantly given a seat on it.[14] The new chair was Maurice Merrill, a labor arbitrator in the oil industry and a law professor from Oklahoma, who had long played a leadership role in the conference and was known for his abilities as a peacemaker. Merrill had no special interest or expertise in matrimonial law, but the others on the committee were attorneys and judges with some involvement in divorce law. In January, 1967, the conference appointed Levy as reporter with the responsibility to provide the committee with drafts and supporting materials. The position gave Levy great influence. Although his recommendations would not win automatic approval, he controlled the agenda and the process by which recommendations to the full conference would be made.

From the very beginning many of those involved in the NCCUSL's effort were inclined to recommend no-fault. Levy himself expressed initial skepticism about the claims no-fault advocates were making. In July of 1967, Levy wrote the executive director of the NCCUSL of his fears that no-fault would not produce the millennium and would just lead to perjury on new matters. "Before acceding to this approach, I would want to make a careful estimate of the number of hard-luck cases the new system is likely to produce, and to compare its malfunctions with those produced by the present system. . . . I wonder how much animosity will be drained from the proceedings, even if the divorce issue is litigated under a noncombative rubric, when salt is freely poured on the wounds as financial matters are determined."[15] Levy was also worried about letting trial judges decide what constitutes marital breakdown. By November, Levy was ready to support a well crafted no-fault provision. He wrote Merrill, "I have (somewhat reluctantly) come into the fold—I am going to recommend that the Conference adopt a Breakdown of Marriage (with safeguards) approach to divorce grounds. My decision has been largely influenced by reading about the European experience with such clauses . . ."[16] From that point onward, the drafts that Levy and his associates prepared included no-fault as the single ground for divorce, although debate about the kinds of safeguards that should accompany no-fault continued. Ten meetings of the committee and the conference followed before the no-fault standard was formally adopted.

Although the NCCUSL's effort began independently of California's endorsement of no-fault divorce, an important link between the two developed during the formulation phase when Herma Hill Kay became co-reporter with Levy in 1968 and played a key role in drafting the uniform law. Kay, however, did not succeed in transferring all of her ideas to the uniform law. Noticeably absent was Kay's family court proposal that had also been dropped in the California legislation. Moreover, the NCCUSL's model law made no mention of conciliation.

On the other hand, the Uniform Marriage and Divorce Act (UMDA) covered many areas not touched by California's efforts; it was a truly comprehensive effort to codify a large portion of family law. Its provisions included innovations in the licensing of marriages and in the handling of annulments; it also sought to codify and reform procedures for handling custody disputes and the division of property upon divorce.

The formulation process within the NCCUSL mirrored California's. It was a four-year process dominated by experts. Although broadly revising the law of marriage and divorce, the drafting committee defined its efforts as technical rather than social reform. Interest groups had little influence; conflict was narrow and framed in a technical manner. There was no media coverage.

Consideration of no-fault divorce by the NCCUSL was even more insulated than the process which had resulted in California's adoption of the idea at the same time. Consider, for instance, the role of the Catholic church. In California, as we have seen, an active line of communication between the governor's commission and a portion of the Catholic hierarchy protected the no-fault proposal from opposition by church conservatives. No evidence exists that the NCCUSL built similar links. A few prominent Catholics were on the drafting committee's advisory board, most notably Father Robert F. Drinan, who seems, however, to have been chosen primarily because of his position with the ABA Family Law Section rather than because he was a Catholic priest. Indeed, he already had a reputation for being something of a maverick among Catholics. There is no evidence in existing documents that church agencies such as the Family Life Bureau of the U.S. Catholic Conference took an active interest in the work of the committee, nor that more than a handful of individual Catholics, even among those on the advisory group, expressed concern.

Two points seem clear from the available record. First, the drafting committee made little effort to obtain support from Catholics or to disarm potential Catholic opposition. Rather, it appeared to assume that the stance of the Catholic church was immaterial, a presumption that appeared well founded, given the lack of Catholic hostility in California toward no-fault divorce. Secondly, no evidence exists that the Catholic national hierarchy paid attention to the work of the drafting committee. In part that may be due to the fact that the Catholic church was oriented to represent its position in Washington and in state capitols but did not monitor the activity of organizations operating elsewhere. Whatever the cause, the consequence was that the church had no voice in the formulation of the UMDA.

Feminists had almost as little influence. No formal link existed between the drafting committee and the National Organization for Women nor with any other feminist organization. Some women who were also feminists were members of the advisory board, most notably Jessie Bernard and Alice Rossi. Neither, however, had been selected because of her feminist connections. The only two exceptions addressing feminist concerns recorded in available documents are to be found in Levy's 1968 monograph, which he wrote as a briefing paper for the drafing committee, and in positions taken by Alice Rossi. In the monograph, during a discussion of property distribution Levy quotes extensively from the 1963 report of the Committee on Civil and Political Rights of the President's Commission on the Status of Women and from the 1968 Task Force on Family Law and Policy of the Citizens' Advisory Council on the Status of Women; his conclusion was that "the time is not yet ripe to insist upon a '50–50' formula," a change he labeled a "radical innovation."[17] However, that was precisely what Rossi urged in her capacity as a member of the advisory group, together with equal consideration of both parents for custody and time-limited alimony. However, having proposed these provisions, she had no success in persuading the predominantly conservative members of the drafting committee to take her suggestions seriously.[18] Thus feminists, like the Catholic church, had little input or influence in the formulation of UMDA.

The insulated position of the conference accentuated the influence of experts in its deliberations. The appellation "expert," of course, can be and was a matter of debate. When the ABA Family Law Section later disputed the conference's proposals, its leaders dismissed Levy and Kay as nothing more than a sociologist and a social worker.[19] Indeed, neither Levy nor Kay had extensively practiced family law. However, both were law professors rather than social scientists and taught family law at their law schools; in addition, Levy was the co-author of a casebook in family law. Thus, their expertise was of a more general and abstract character than that of many of the members of the Family Law Section whose proficiency rested mostly on the law of the particular state in which they practiced.

With this general expertise, which in Kay's instance was buttressed by her experience in formulating California's no-fault divorce statute, the reporters directed the work of the drafting committee. They wrote the drafts which committee members then commented upon and debated. The debates were sometimes heated[20] and the reporters did not always win their point, as shown by their failure to carry the issue of limiting judicial discretion where the greater caution and conservatism of the committee members prevailed. Likewise, Levy failed to carry the committee with him on his preferences with respect to child custody sections of the model law. These were exceptions, however. It can be fairly said that UMDA bore the clear marks of Levy's and Kay's authorship.

Adoption by the conference came after a long debate in which the commissioners examined each paragraph.[21] As in the original formulation of the problem, the debate over the proposed solution used the language of legal technical terms rather than of social concepts and issues.[22] The debate transcripts rarely display an articulated concern over such matters as the fate of divorced women or the differential impact of the law's provisions on minority groups or the poor. When commissioners had such concerns, they couched them in technical terms. That is well illustrated in the debate over whether judges should possess discretion over the granting of a divorce on the ground of matrimonial breakdown. Both in the drafting committee and during the debate by the conference as a whole, enormous attention was lavished on whether the statute should include the word "may" or "shall." At the manifest level it was an abstract, constitutional debate on judicial discretion and judicial power. However, the discussion reflected several, mostly unspoken, social issues. The debate over judicial discretion was also an argument over whether marital misbehavior should go unpunished; however, if judges retained discretion to deny divorces to persons who had acted badly in their marriage, fault would reenter through the back door. In addition, this discussion may have reflected disquiet over the possibility that judges might deny divorces to the poor,[23] but it also betrayed a concern over the potential for increased welfare costs as well as a regard for equal treatment under the law. At the manifest level, the debate in the conference did not focus on social issues but rather concentrated on the judicial authority denoted by those two words and on the legal definition of irretrievable breakdown.

The technical character of the conference's debate reflected its structure and composition. It was not a representative body and its members did not have to answer to a constituency. Many were law professors who were comfortable in discussing legal technicalities. Neither interest groups nor reporters intervened to raise questions of social conflict. Furthermore, the technical cast of the debates also helped insulate the deliberations from the media. Media representatives were not routinely invited to conference sessions or to the meetings of the drafting committees. Thus the media were usually unaware of the conference's activities. However, even if they had been aware, conference debates would have provided poor copy and a pale television image because the commissioners did not speak the language of political conflict. Even the later dispute with the ABA produced only minimal coverage which failed to capture the essence of the differences between the two organizations.

By the time the NCCUSL debated its committee's proposal, California had already acted. When skeptics in the conference debate asked whether no-fault was practical or inquired about the opposition of the Catholic church, supporters were able to point to the California experience, where no-fault had been adopted under a conservative governor without active Catholic opposition.

None of the issues raised during the discussion seriously threatened the proposal, and it easily passed the NCCUSL to become the Uniform Marriage and Divorced Act in the terminology of the conference. At that juncture, however, the routine procedures governing such proposals required expanding the list of participants to the American Bar Association's House of Delegates. That group reflected somewhat different concerns and for three years blocked the UMDA's final approval.

The ABA's failure to ratify the NCCUSL's actions reflected several consequences of this broadening of the arena. The ABA had a Family Law Section which was run by a combination of practitioners and academics. The practitioners feared the consequences of the proposed changes on their accustomed routines; the academics felt slighted by their treatment from the NCCUSL.

Part of the problem lay in the clash of personalities. Levy's appointment was a fateful one. While partisan and interest group politics played no role in the NCCUSL's and ABA's deliberations, they were not immune from the warp of intramural politics. From the very beginning, jealousy and organizational suspicion marked the relationship between the NCCUSL's drafting committee and the ABA Family Law Section and their two respective leaders, Robert Levy and Henry H. Foster, Jr. While the conflict between the ABA and the NCCUSL was always argued on substantive rather than personal grounds, the personality clash seems to have contributed to it. For instance, Levy wrote in 1973:

The very existence of the Family Law Section liaison committee was from the beginning a source of controversy. Chairman Merrill was convinced that a liaison committee would help to purchase support for the Act from the American Bar Association. Mrs. Merrill, a Special Committee Advisor, and the Reporter both opposed creation of such a committee because its membership might include persons disaffected by the Conference's selection of paid staff and because the committee would not be able to assuage its resentment that the Conference rather than the Family Law Section had responsibility for drafting the Act.[24]

Another observer of this conflict wrote:

. . . personal relationships play a large part in the molding of public policy as do ideas and concepts. After discussing the problem with many of the participants in the dispute, there is no doubt in my mind that had the relationship between the Commissioners and reporter on the one hand and the members of the Family Law Section liaison committee on the other been a good one, no competing draft would have been prepared. Nearly everyone involved wanted progressive legislation but that goal was very nearly thwarted by the hostility of the two groups toward each other.[25]

Consultation between the Family Law Section and the NC-CUSL drafting committee was rocky at best. The Family Law Section had been formed slightly more than ten years earlier; its members justifiably felt that they had been kept at the periphery of the ABA and were piqued that the NCCUSL had taken the lead role in formulating reform. Some of its old-time leaders, such as Clarence Kolwyck, were quite hostile to sociologically inclined academics such as Levy and Kay;[26] indeed, Family Law Section's liaison committee to the NC-CUSL's drafting committee perceived Levy and Kay as starry-eyed idealists with no practical background in family law matters.[27]

Although the Family Law Section did not object to irretrievable breakdown as the ground for divorce, they considered its implementation in UMDA as too radical, as unlikely to win approval by state legislatures, and as possessing dangerous ambiguities in its failure to list criteria for marital breakdown. The ABA opponents even engaged in red-baiting in their attack on UMDA; the chair of the Family Law Section, Henry Foster, wrote that both England and Canada had rejected irretrievable breakdown as the sole standard for divorce "perhaps because the only legal precedent for an exclusive breakdown ground was that of Soviet Russia. . . ."[28] The Family Law Section opposed what Foster called "administrative divorce upon request,"[29] and feared that the UMDA would encourage unilateral divorce actions where the simple allegation of marital breakdown by one partner would inevitably lead to divorce, with no protection for the other partner and no way for a judge to avoid issuing the divorce decree.[30]

Consequently, the UMDA was rejected by the ABA in 1970 after it was proposed by the NCCUSL. This action was so unusual that it attracted brief notice from some national newspapers and news magazines. The rejection, however, was not final. Negotiations began between the Family Law Section and the NCCUSL's drafting committee, from which both Levy and Kay (the key experts) were excluded. The negotiations resulted in some relatively minor changes in the UMDA, such as a ninety-day waiting period between a couple's separation and the granting of a divorce in place of the Family Law Section's desired specification of the meaning of irretrievable breakdown.[31] Those changes, nevertheless, sparked considerable debate within the NCCUSL, with many members expressing anger over the Family Law Section's attempt to dictate to the NCCUSL; after venting those feelings, however, the NCCUSL's members agreed to the revisions.[32] The Family Law Section then also relented and the House of Delegates of the ABA endorsed the revised model statute in 1974.

With ABA approval achieved, the Uniform Marriage and Divorce Act became a model for state legislatures to emulate. Newspapers duly noted that no-fault divorce was now advocated by lawyers. The UMDA was published by the NCCUSL and distributed to each of its commissioners and sent to every state legislature. A handful of articles on the UMDA appeared in law journals. It was hardly a great event and, as we shall see in the next chapter, it had little immediate impact on the widespread adoption of no-fault divorce in the United States. Its most important effect was to legitimate no-fault in a way that California's adoption could not. Whereas California's adoption might be discounted because California often adopted avant-garde ideas belittled elsewhere, the NCCUSL and ABA's endorsement of no-fault divorce indicated that this was a reasonable idea that warranted serious consideration by state legislatures, for the NCCUSL and ABA were middle-of-the-road, conservative organizations little given to extravagant social experimentation.

Conclusion

The routine policy-making process within the NCCUSL and ABA was different from California's in one significant characteristic: their decisions had only the status of recommendations to the states rather than of laws with potentially irreversible effects. However, these groups undertook their tasks with great seriousness, believing that the reputations of their organizations were at stake in adopting model laws that could win the respect of the nation's lawmakers. Thus their actions were not without the risk and uncertainty that California legislators also faced.

What made divorce reform an attractive object for the routine policy process was the ability of its advocates to formulate the problem as a matter which required special expertise more than broad public participation. As in California, the reformers did not portray no-fault as a daring experiment but rather as a logical extension of existing practices. The NCCUSL's procedures guaranteed limited visibility among the general public and confined decision making to inside experts until the proposals were transmitted to the ABA. Ordinarily, the NCCUSL would have coopted the relevant ABA experts as well and its proposals would have been routinely adopted by the association. That did not occur with the Uniform Marriage and Divorce Act, as we saw, because of personal and institutional rivalries. Nevertheless, the proponents of reform succeeded in confining conflict to the private arenas of the decision-making processes of the two groups, where a compromise was reached in typically technical terms. They did not allow the issue to become transformed into a social conflict which would have invited other groups and members of the general public to intervene.

As in California, vigorous advocacy by dedicated reformers within an institutional dynamic marked the routine policy process in the NCCUSL. Hellring and Brown mobilized the Conference to obtain the necessary funds to proceed, whereupon the inertial force of the Conference's procedures took over. Without Hellring and Brown's insistence, it seems doubtful that the leadership of the conference would have placed marriage and divorce on their agenda. The history of the conference was too blemished with failures in this field, and there was little indication that it would succeed in the 1960s when it had floundered so often in the past. Moreover, it would have been impossible for the conference to proceed without its grant from the Ford Foundation because it did not possess sufficient funds of its own to finance the appointment of a reporter and the meetings of the drafting commission. Thus a small foundation donation reinforced the efforts of the initial reformers.

Thereafter, the conference imposed its routine procedures to the process. It appointed a drafting committee with responsibility to report back to the conference in a timely fashion. The executive director of the conference and his office served as a clearing house for the committee and monitored its progress. The replacement of the policy entrepreneurs with the organizational technocrat, Merrill, was another force for keeping the project moving because Merrill was an experienced commissioner who had served in leadership positions and knew the conference's routine thoroughly. Levy and Kay then set the agenda and wrote the drafts upon which committee deliberations focused. The annual meeting of the conference served as a mechanism for regulating the schedule of the committee's work. Levy, Kay, Merrill, and other members of the drafting committee had a stake in seeing the task to completion. These elements provided strong organizational support for concluding the task of drafting a uniform marriage and divorce code which had begun through the advocacy of policy entrepreneurs.

6

The Vagaries of Diffusion

No-fault divorce spread like a prairie fire. By 1974, the year in which the National Conference of Commissioners on Uniform State Laws (NCCUSL) and the American Bar Association (ABA) had promulgated the Uniform Marriage and Divorce Act (UMDA) with its no-fault provisions, the most authoritative listing of state divorce laws declared that forty-five states already possessed a no-fault procedure.[1] The five states where fault remained the sole basis for a divorce were slow to join the rush to no-fault, but by 1985 the last, South Dakota, had enlisted under the no-fault banner. That was a remarkable achievement, considering the formidable obstacles that the fragmented American political system puts in the way of winning adoption of any policy from each of the fifty states. Moreover, these adoptions occurred during a decade widely bemoaned as a period of political paralysis and stalemate.

The diffusion of no-fault resembles an Impressionist painting. At a distance, it appears to be composed of broad strokes forming a single wave, but on closer examination it stands revealed as a series of discrete and apparently unrelated acts.

Only fifteen of the states eliminated all fault provisions in their divorce code and permitted divorce solely on the allegation of an irretrievable breakdown of the marriage.[2] The remaining thirty-five states simply added some form of no-fault to their existing divorce codes, giving couples a choice between obtaining their divorce on the basis of irretrievable breakdown or using one of the traditional grounds such as cruelty or adultery.

Moreover, some of these thirty-five states never embraced no-fault by an explicit legislative act but had for many years possessed provisions that resembled no-fault. One such state was Arkansas, which in 1937 passed a law that permitted divorce after a separation of three years.[3] Another was Oklahoma, which adopted incompatibility as a ground for divorce in 1953.[4] Since 1957, Texas had permitted divorce on grounds of separation without proof of a fault ground.[5] None of these states had explicitly considered the no-fault concept when they adopted these provisions. In addition, twenty states adopted separation as a ground for divorce after no-fault became fashionable.[6] The length of the separation could be as short as six months (in Vermont) or as long as five years (Rhode Island).[7] In some instances, states intentionally accepted separation as a no-fault ground for divorce. In others, however, no explicit discussion about no-fault divorce marked the adoption of separation as a ground for divorce. That was most apparent, as we have seen, in New York, where the 1966 reforms allowed a two-year separation to be converted into a divorce; the two years were cut to one in 1970. If no-fault was on the minds of the drafters of that legislation, they carefully disguised their intentions; no-fault was simply not part of the political vocabulary in New York when those changes were contemplated.

Many of the twenty states with separation as a ground for divorce became no-fault states not through the action of their legislature and not even through a decision by their supreme court. Rather, they came to be included among the no-fault jurisdictions on the basis of a 1974 listing in the journal of the Family Law Section, the *Family Law Quarterly*.[8] That listing, and its subsequent updates, became the authoritative catalogue of divorce statutes in the United States. The authors' characterization of states like Missouri and South Carolina as possessing no-fault despite the lack of explicit legislative or judicial action aroused no visible objection. It undoubtedly reflected the character of the law-in-action if not the specific words of the statute, and thus it became part of the conventional wisdom that those states possessed no-fault divorce. Consequently, almost as soon as the NCCUSL and ABA had ratified the no-fault model law, a decisive majority of states were declared to possess it.

Such a bold attempt to legislate by scholarly fiat in a law journal would probably have failed if no-fault had been controversial or contrary to the drift of legislation in other states. In fact, as we have already seen for California, no-fault attracted little opposition. In addition, a growing number of state legislatures explicitly embraced the concept.

The spread of no-fault is not unprecedented in the annals of American policy making, although the rapidity of no-fault's acceptance was unusual. Typically, innovations are pioneered by one state or another and then win gradual acceptance by most of the others, although the diffusion normally requires many decades. Consequently, even though each state is master over its own statute book, the laws of the states bear a close resemblance to one another. Only a handful of themes are represented in each area of law, with many states composing their own variations to suit local preferences.

Innovation and diffusion have attracted considerable scholarly attention with several kinds of analyses. One focuses on creativity and the circumstances which lead to the initial invention of a policy.[9] A second focuses on the pattern of emulation and the circumstances which appear to be associated with it.[10] Thus some scholars have pointed to social movements as the carriers of new policies, and surely they sometimes are. Others have emphasized the role of interest groups in advocating common policies across state lines. Still others point to the role of bureaucratic networks in transferring not only technology but also programmatic ideas.[11] Other bodies of research have stressed the centrality of political entrepreneurs or resource availability in promoting the adoption of innovations. The residual explanation often simply is the ripeness of circumstances. We shall explore each of these alternatives and then examine the experiences of three emulating states to search for a more plausible explanation of no-fault's quick approval across the nation.

Divorce Reform as the Product of a Social Movement

Social movements, defined as widespread, organized public support for policy change, have been associated with some of the more spectacular changes in American public policy in the twentieth century. Prohibition was the product of a well-orchestrated public outcry to ban King Rum from the land.[12] The Civil Rights Acts of the 1960s were the outcome of the civil rights movement that began with freedom marches in the South and ended as a nationwide popular outcry to improve the legal position of blacks in American society.[13] The tax revolt of the 1970s which led many jurisdictions to adopt property tax limitations had a similarly broad base of grievances and organized activity.[14]

It is difficult to find evidence for a social movement generating no-fault divorce. As we have seen for New York, California, and the NCCUSL, no-fault legislation flourished in deep shade far from the glare of public attention. One indication of this is that public opinion polls rarely asked about divorce. Although one can find single poll questions about divorce laws in 1936, 1945, 1954, and 1966,[15] the issue was apparently not pressing enough to justify more frequent polling. None of the questions mentioned no-fault. The 1945 poll revealed that while four-fifths of the respondents supported the abstract ideal of uniformity in divorce laws, only 9% thought existing divorce laws were too strict.[16] Twenty-one years later that number had risen by only four percentage points, close to the margin of error for such a poll.[17] Moreover, in that same 1966 poll, the proportion reporting no opinion rose from 25 to 35%, while only 25% supported a two-year separation as ground for divorce, the choice closest to true no-fault permitted by the poll.[18] In the 1970s and early 1980s, support for easier divorce laws was higher—in the range of one-third of the sample—but unlike the responses to the earlier polls, a majority by 1982 thought divorce laws should become stricter.[19] These data clearly indicate that no massive public support existed for tinkering with divorce laws, and that public opinion polls provided no mandate for adopting no-fault divorce.

Nor did any of the other public activities associated with social movements exist. No one organized public protests, marches, or sit-ins against fault grounds. In the context of the turmoil of the 1960s, protest against existing divorce laws simply was not visible.

Moreover, no mass organizations sprang up to champion no-fault divorce. There was no analogue of the Women's Christian Temperance Union or the many groups of the civil rights movement. Aside from the NCCUSL and family law sections of bar associations, it was difficult to find a group with no-fault divorce on its agenda, and those groups were, of course, not mass organizations but professional associations composed of attorneys.

There was, however, another mass movement stirring while no-fault divorce progressed through state legislatures—the feminist movement. It was revitalized after a hiatus of almost a generation following the adoption of the Nineteenth Amendment to the Constitution granting women the vote in 1920. In 1966 the National Organization for Women was created and it quickly became the largest organization of feminists, while *MS Magazine* became a mass circulation outlet for the movement. Feminists achieved congressional approval of the Equal Rights Amendment (ERA) in 1972, which was then sent to the states for ratification. Feminists spoke loudly and clearly for equal rights; they staged demonstrations and spawned not just NOW but a galaxy of smaller organizations.[20]

The feminist movement paralleled the earlier efforts of the civil rights movement, particularly in its focus on consciousness raising as one of its major goals so that Americans would become aware of gender as a source of illegitimate discrimination. It succeeded in that effort to an astonishing degree with the inclusion of sex as an illegal basis of job discrimination in the Civil Rights Act of 1964, before NOW was even organized,[21] with subsequent court decisions enforcing that legislation, with the widespread acceptance of the appellation Ms. for women who did not want to be identified by their marital status, and with a sweeping movement to make laws neutral with respect to gender, among many other changes.

However, no-fault divorce was not part of the feminist

agenda. Neither in California nor in the deliberations of the NCCUSL was the feminist voice raised. As we saw in the previous chapter, individual feminists articulated some concern during the drafting of the Uniform Marriage and Divorce Act but were unsuccessful in having their views adopted. No-fault divorce was mentioned in some feminist documents, but it never became an issue which attracted the vigorous support of feminists or of movement organizations. Although some feminists viewed no-fault with suspicion, fearing that the change would work to the detriment of divorcing wives, that opinion rarely blossomed into explicit opposition. Thus, while a social movement existed which might have championed no-fault, it did not do so.[22]

No-fault divorce, like many other changes in American public policy, was not the result of a massive social movement. It won acceptance on other grounds.

Interest Groups

Most descriptions of contemporary American politics assign a very large role to interest groups in the formulation and revision of public policy.[23] Almost since its beginning, the United States has been known for the abundance of groups seeking to represent every conceivable interest in society.

Interest groups were not entirely absent during the consideration of no-fault divorce as it spread through the states. However, the range of groups requesting a hearing was very limited. In most states, only lawyers and the Catholic church paid attention to no-fault legislation. In addition, small groups purporting to represent fathers or men more generally emerged intermittently to lend support to no-fault legislation; their concern was to remove divorce entirely from the courts, and they perceived no-fault divorce as a step in this direction.[24] Such groups organized on a local basis and were tiny in comparison to their potential membership.[25] However, they were sometimes strident witnesses at legislative hearings that were otherwise void of group representation except for that provided by bar associations and the Catholic church.

Bar associations participated in the revision process in almost every state.[26] In some like Arizona,[27] Connecticut,[28] and Washington,[29] they participated in the drafting of the no-fault law and supported the change. In others, however, the family law section used the occasion to limit change, as in Michigan[30] and Maine,[31] where it opposed including alterations in property distribution in the no-fault law. In every state, the bar routinely screens proposed legislation because almost every new law affects its work. As a consequence, however, divorce reform had to compete with many other matters on the bar's agenda, and it usually occupied a place well below other, more urgently pressed items.

Two other characteristics of bar efforts to promote no-fault divorce were significant. First, the segment of the legal profession handling many divorces was outside the leadership circle of most bar associations because divorce lawyers were generally among the lower status attorneys. Elite lawyers tried to avoid entanglement in divorce cases and would openly boast that they had never needed to handle one. It was also an area of low specialization; most lawyers regarded divorce as something that any attorney could handle. Thus the divorce lawyers coming to the state capitol to comment on no-fault divorce proposals did not command especially high respect from legislators. Indeed, often those legislators who were lawyers had themselves handled divorces and did not regard the family law section representatives as more qualified than they themselves were.

Secondly, family law practitioners did not unanimously endorse no-fault divorce. Some raised the specter of a massive wave of divorces if their state abandoned fault grounds. Others feared the loss of business to do-it-yourself divorce kits if divorce law became too simple.[32] Still others resisted (in most cases successfully) the wholesale revision of their state's divorce laws because it would require extensive retooling on their part. Consequently, the state bar rarely was the dominant voice in the consideration of no-fault divorce.

The Catholic church was the second large group which sometimes articulated a position on no-fault divorce. In principle the church opposed divorce entirely, but it had learned to accommodate itself to the widespread availability of divorce in the United States which existed before the church became a force on the American political scene. Nevertheless, the church hierarchy feared that divorce would become too easy if fault grounds were abandoned. These crosscurrents led to variable activity by the church. In states where it was not a major player in the political game it kept silent, preferring to concentrate on issues more salient to its current concerns, such as abortion or state aid to parochial schools. However, in states with large Catholic populations, the church expressed more vigorous opposition. It is surely no accident that many of the states with large Catholic populations were late adopters of no-fault. Thus, Massachusetts and Rhode Island accepted it in 1975, Pennsylvania in 1980, and Illinois in 1983. New York, as we have already indicated, never explicitly adopted no-fault. As we shall see below, the Catholic church sometimes exerted strong pressure to avert no-fault. Ultimately, of course, it failed as no-fault became the national standard.

Conspicuously absent from the legislative arena was the National Conference of Commissioners on Uniform State Laws. Every state had several commissioners, each of whom had a formal obligation to promote the conference's uniform laws, but there is little indication that they played a leading role in suggesting no-fault to their states. Indeed, as we have seen, a majority of states were deemed to possess no-fault divorce by the time the NCCUSL and ABA agreed on the Uniform Marriage and Divorce Act. Nevertheless, the states would have needed to adopt much of the model act if divorce law were to become more uniform throughout the nation; yet few states adopted large segments of the UMDA and none adopted it without some change. The promulgation of the UMDA with its no-fault provisions undoubtedly legitimized no-fault divorce, and the NCCUSL statute served as a model for state legislative reference bureaus and statute-drafting agencies. However, there is no sign that the NCCUSL actively lobbied for the UMDA. Neither Levy nor Kay testified extensively before state legislatures in its behalf. Nor did other members of the drafting committee or the legislative director.[33]

Thus interest groups played only a small role in the diffusion of no-fault divorce. One cannot attribute its quick acceptance to the concerted effort of any single group or coalition of groups. At most, interest groups generally indicated that no-

fault divorce was an acceptable idea, a reform safe for legislators to endorse.

Diffusion Networks

Observers of the diffusion of policy innovations usually attribute the spread of an innovation to the activity of sponsoring
organizations, and to the dissemination of knowledge about
the innovation through specialized journals and personal contacts.[34] To some extent, such activity existed in the case of no-
fault divorce. The endorsement of no-fault by the NCCUSL
and the ABA made it much more widely known than it might
otherwise have been. Specialized legal periodicals gave increasing attention to no-fault.[35] Some articles may have been
particularly influential. For instance, Henry Foster brought no-
fault to the attention of specialists in an article summarizing
the California Governor's Commission and the English no-
fault proposals in the first issue of the *Family Law Quarterly* in
1967.[36] Likewise, the Foote, Levy, and Sander casebook on
family law discussed the idea.[37]

However, two diffusion agents often prominent in the
spread of innovations were absent in the case of no-fault divorce. The first was a government bureaucracy.[38] Most other
public policies are administered by agencies that often play a
conspicuous role in promoting or opposing change. For instance, no educational reform can be considered without
hearing from school superintendents, state universities, state
departments of education, and the federal department of education. Such agencies normally participate in personal and
professional networks through which information flows, or
they may dispense incentives to promote a new policy. Sometimes they share or exchange personnel; in other instances they
trade annual reports which include information about innovative procedures just adopted. In the divorce arena, however,
no bureaucratic linkages existed because no agency processes
divorces except courts; and the courts of a state are rarely
linked to the judiciary of others in the same manner as administrative agencies are. Moreover, courts seldom enter the
legislative arena to advocate change except for alterations in
judicial structure.[39] Indeed, only when reformers threatened

the organizational integrity of existing courts with the addition of a family court did the judiciary normally become active, but in opposition to the change.

The second change agent usually absent from the consideration of no-fault divorce was the specialist who attends professional conventions to exchange current ideas. Every professional group has its national and regional meetings which serve that purpose. Only the bar worked in this fashion with respect to no-fault divorce, and its meetings undoubtedly aided the diffusion process. However, the lawyers who attended those meetings were usually outsiders to the policy-making process, in contrast to bureaucratic specialists who come home from their meetings to propose an innovation to their agency chief, who may in turn take it directly to the governor or legislature.

Thus the diffusion network so evident in the spread of other innovations was much weaker in the case of no-fault divorce. It was not entirely absent, but it did not play a vigorous role.

Political Entrepreneurship

The old-fashioned term is leadership, and it is often used to explain changes in public policy.[40] The legislative process requires sponsorship of a bill: the agendas of most legislatures are so crowded that bills do not become laws unless someone pushes for their adoption. When a proposal attracts wide attention, formal leaders in the political arena exercise that function, as when a governor makes a proposal part of his program or when the presiding officer of a legislative chamber or the chairperson of the relevent committee embraces the proposal and gives it the weight of their endorsement.

Proposals for no-fault divorce did not escape the necessity of political sponsorship. However, formal leaders rarely became involved in the early stages during the formulation of the bill. In no state is there evidence that no-fault divorce became part of the governor's legislative program. The benign neutrality of Governor Rockefeller in New York and Governor Reagan in California was, as we have seen, important for no-fault's legislative passage and, of course, essential for its becoming law, since the governor had to sign the bill (or at least not veto it). In New York, divorce reform involved the leadership of the legislature because it was perceived as politically delicate, but leaders became involved only after a political entrepreneur pushed it onto the legislative agenda with his vigorous advocacy and coalition building efforts. In California, advocacy came from committee chairs in the state assembly and senate.

This pattern was repeated throughout the nation as no-fault bills were considered by legislatures in the 1970s. In some instances, leadership came from legislative sponsors who perceived no-fault as an instrument to build their reputation at little risk. They regarded no-fault as an innovation that was sweeping the country and saw an opportunity to bring their state onto the bandwagon. In most instances these entrepreneurs were members of the legislature, but in a few they were outsiders. Sometimes leadership came from chairs of legislative committees who picked no-fault from the list of bills being considered by their committees because they became aware of the national trend and did not wish to see their state as a laggard. The fact that the proposal roused little opposition added to the attractiveness of sponsorship.

In few states, however, was no-fault a conspicuous example of political leadership or entrepreneurship. It did not generally become a vehicle to build political careers. The contrast with abortion legislation in California is instructive. The sponsor of the bill liberalizing abortion that was considered at approximately the same time was a freshman member of the state general assembly, and he used the prominence gained from his sponsorship to advance to Congress.[41] By contrast, the assembly sponsor of the no-fault divorce bill moved to Los Angeles county politics and then dropped out of public sight; the senate sponsor remained in the senate but did not consider no-fault as one of his major achievements.[42] Moreover, no one involved in the no-fault legislation was interviewed for the oral history of the Reagan administration in California.[43] Political entrepreneurs played only a small role in Iowa as well; no one remembers who was responsible for pushing no-fault through the legislature and contemporary records fail to identify its principal advocate.[44] On the other hand, Illinois's 1977 no-fault legislation[45] is clearly attributed to one attorney who pushed his version through the legislature, even though he was not a member; his role is memorialized in the historical note to the legislation which he wrote and which continues to be printed in the annotated code of Illinois. The legislative sponsors are also well remembered.[46]

Thus, leadership clearly played a role in no-fault's spread, but it was not the dominant factor in most states. No-fault did not have sufficient prominence to promise large political dividends for its sponsors. Nonetheless, the lack of vocal opposition in most states made it a low-risk venture which might add to the reputation of a legislator even if it were not a sure vehicle for promotion.

Resource Availability

Some theories of innovation posit that innovations are more likely to win acceptance when the organization considering them has slack resources, because new procedures and activities usually require additional resources.[47] If resources are scarce, the innovation must compete with existing demands; if they are plentiful, the innovation may be adopted without arousing opposition from adherents of established policies. Empirically, it has been noted that many innovations in public policy appear to be adopted first by wealthy states which presumably have more resource slack, although many exceptions exist.[48] For instance, Wisconsin, which is not notably wealthy, for many years shared as innovative a tradition as California, which has the reputation for both daring and wealth. Likewise, such poor states as Mississippi are by no means always among the last to adopt innovative procedures. Clearly more is involved than simply the wealth of a state.

Part of the problem with the conventional formulation of the resource hypothesis lies in equating wealth with slack resources. It is quite plausible that wealthy states have all their resources committed and therefore have little or no slack for adopting innovations, while a poorer state has more slack because of a sudden upturn in revenues or because of greater administrative efficiency.

Moreover, not all innovations require resources. The cost-free character of no-fault divorce was one of its attractive features. If it was not accompanied by counseling services or family courts, no-fault divorce did not cost the states a cent. As we have already seen for California, the proposal for establishing a costly new tier of family courts was what attracted most opposition to the no-fault bill, and when its sponsors abandoned this feature, the bill sailed to easy passage. Likewise, counseling services in New York were soon dropped after having been initially added as a concession to those who feared easy divorces would lead to increased marital disruption.

When no-fault stood by itself, it had no implications for the state budget. Moreover, this was accomplished without shifting costs to the private sector, as is the case with such programs as the Food and Drug Administration's labeling requirements. No one argued that no-fault divorces would be more expensive to obtain; indeed, some made the opposite argument. Thus the resource hypothesis has little plausibility in the case of no-fault.

The record of no-fault adoptions also shows little relationship between the wealth of states and the date of their acceptance of the idea. As we have already noted, Arkansas and Oklahoma were among very early embracers of the substance of the no-fault idea if not of its explicit provisions, and they stood near the bottom of the list of states in terms of their wealth. Among the early adopters of pure no-fault who eliminated all fault alternatives were not only California, but also Iowa in 1970, Colorado, Florida, Michigan, and Oregon in 1971, and Kentucky and Nebraska in 1972, many of which were not among the most wealthy states. And while four of these states rank among the eight most innovative states in Walker's study, the other four rank below the median.[49]

The Time Was Ripe

In the absence of another compelling explanation, it is perhaps plausible to argue that no-fault became nearly universal simply because the time was ripe for such a measure. As we have seen in earlier chapters, much evidence seems to support such an explanation. Divorce rates were on the rise and divorce had become more acceptable to the American population; by 1976, an overwhelming majority of both men and women thought that divorce was "often" the best solution to an unsatisfactory marriage.[50] Divorce had also become so common that many people had either experienced it themselves or witnessed it among relatives, friends, or acquaintances. Thus the barrier that social stigma had raised in earlier decades was crumbling, and the argument that no-fault might make divorce too easy lost much of its force.

Moreover, some women thought divorce a more realistic alternative in economic terms than had formerly been true. The rhetoric of the women's movement, the promise of Title 7 of the 1964 Civil Rights Act, and the fact that far more women held paying jobs may have led some women to expect that they could support themselves and their children without the help of their husbands. That too made no-fault divorce more attractive because it promised quicker dissolution of unhappy marriages without the conflict associated with conventional divorces.

As we have already noted, no-fault was also becoming popularized in the field of automobile accident insurance. Its spread in the personal injury field undoubtedly lent the idea legitimacy in the divorce field.

However, there is no way of confirming the "time is ripe" explanation because it is non-falsifiable. It may be plausible to assert that policies win acceptance because the time is ripe, but when is the time not ripe? The only evidence against the explanation is that a policy is rejected. The acceptance or rejection of a policy thus becomes the indicator of the ripeness of the times—which is then used to explain the fate of the policy proposal. The circular nature of this argument makes it unacceptable as an explanation for the acceptance or rejection of a policy.

In rejecting the "time is ripe" explanation, however, one must not ignore the supportive social environment which may have asssisted the spread of no-fault. Such circumstances constitute a necessary but not sufficient explanation for the spread of a policy. It would have been infinitely more difficult to promote no-fault in the absence of job opportunities for divorced women, in the face of severe social stigma for divorcees, or in opposition to public opinion about divorce. However, a supportive social environment only permits political agents to work for change; it does not produce the change itself. It was in that sense that the ripe social conditions contributed to the spread of no-fault divorce without being a full explanation in themselves.

The Emulation Process in Three States

No single factor emerges to explain the rapid diffusion of no-fault. Different combinations of factors had varying significance, as can be illustrated by examining in greater detail the emulation process in particular states. We shall look at three. Iowa is an example of a very early emulator of California; Wisconsin made its decision in the middle; and Illinois was a late acceptor. Each shows a different combination of the factors we have outlined above.

Iowa

Iowa was the second state to adopt no-fault as the only criteria for obtaining a divorce. It followed California by one year. But its path to no-fault was quite different.[51]

In late 1967, a group of legislators signed a petition seeking a committee to study Iowa divorce laws while the legislature was recessed. The petition noted "that the statutes of the State of Iowa are in some respects outmoded and deficient by modern sociological standards."[52] That statement appeared to refer to the therapeutic theories about marital disruption, because the signatories thought that alterations in Iowa's divorce laws would reduce the divorce rate and minimize the bad effects of those divorces which did occur. Consequently, they suggested mandatory counseling, a mandatory 120-day waiting period, appointment of an attorney for children, and changing the standards for granting alimony. Their petition made no mention of no-fault divorce.

The committee that was appointed drifted toward no-fault. Its first meeting in mid-April focused on counseling and what to do if counseling failed. At the second meeting there was a discussion of the harmful effects of adversarial divorces, the proverbial messy trials at which all the dirty laundry of a marriage was hung out for public view. The third meeting focused on child custody and child support issues. Not until the fourth meeting did a committee member who was also a judge propose eliminating consideration of fault in the distribution of property. Finally, at the fifth meeting this judge proposed having the court consider dissolution of marriage after sixty days if conciliation failed. Under his proposal, the original divorce petition would not specify grounds, but only state that grounds for divorce existed; if a respondent wanted to learn what the grounds were, he or she would have to use a discovery motion. At the same time, this committee member suggested substituting the word dissolution for divorce.

During the committee's discussion, it was clear that the judge had California's proposals in mind even though they had not yet been adopted. In addition, the committee had been given copies of the Archbishop of Canterbury's report, which advocated a limited form of no-fault divorce. From this point onward, no-fault became embedded in the committee's draft, although the term itself was never mentioned in the committee's minutes or its report. The committee's final report submitted in November 1968 recommended repealing all grounds for divorce and substituting an irretrievable breakdown standard. The report also recommended compulsory counseling and the establishment of separate family courts for the state.

The committee operated in deeper obscurity than California's legislative study committees or its governor's commission. It heard no public witnesses; its meetings were not noted in the media. It was not the product of an identifiable reform group and no single member or group is remembered as having been the driving force behind its work. It was loosely connected to the meager informational network on divorce law through its dependence on the Iowa Legislative Reference Service for staff assistance. That agency, which had just been organized, provided committee members with considerable information about divorce laws and proposals in other states. On the other hand, no evidence exists that the committee worked with the Iowa Bar Association or with the University of Iowa Law School specialists in family law. On the day it submitted its report America's astronauts landed on the moon for the second time; the committee's report was not mentioned by Des Moines's two newspapers.[53]

The legislative history of the committee's recommendations is shrouded in the mists of forgotten events. They were not taken up by the legislature in 1969. The bar and bench opposed the family court proposal and, as in California, it was dropped by the legislature because of its cost. The bill then won widespread bipartisan support and encountered no organized opposition. In the lower house, the majority leader managed it on the floor. It passed both houses by overwhelming margins and was swiftly signed by the governor. Its passage was noted in front-page stories in the *Des Moines Register,* but that was the only time the bill was mentioned in the newspapers.[54]

The ease with which no-fault became law in Iowa suggests the power of a favorable environment and the effectiveness of the low-profile strategy its advocates followed. No interest-group activity on either side of the question is now discernible. No one seems to have played a significant leadership role. The information network was tapped but it could not give strong cues, since only California and England were at the time considering no-fault divorce. There is no indication that Iowa's committee was aware of the deliberations of the NCCUSL, which were only at the drafting committee stage and had produced no official document that states could copy. Nor did Iowa officials give much consideration to the potential consequences of no-fault. They sponsored no research and heard no testimony. Drift is the best descriptor for Iowa's experience.

Illinois

Neighboring Illinois passed a divorce bill seven years after Iowa, and both the politics and the resulting bill were entirely different.[55] As in Iowa, feminists were invisible, but the Catholic church exercised decisive influence while the legal profession was split. Moreover, a single policy entrepreneur played a prominent role. Conflict was visible and well reported by the media, although the effort to bring no-fault to the state did not become a major political issue. The result was a peculiar law which eliminated fault for everything except the divorce itself. Consequently, marital offenses could no longer be cited in Illinois with respect to the division of property or to decisions about child custody, but they continued to be necessary for obtaining the divorce. As is true of much of Illinois politics, the course of this divorce bill was byzantine.

Illinois divorce law had remained essentially unchanged since 1874. At the time of its adoption, the 1874 law was clearly in the mainstream of American divorce practice by requiring that a marital offense be proved and that the divorce be granted to the innocent party. Divorce was not available after a period of voluntary separation as it was in a growing number of states.

After the pioneering example of California as well as that of neighboring Iowa, and the promulgation of the UMDA by the NCCUSL which had its offices in Chicago, legislators introduced a number of no-fault bills into the General Assembly in the early 1970s. Until 1977 they were not taken seriously because the Catholic church opposed them. The church's lobbying arm, the Illinois Catholic Conference, was widely respected as a powerful lobby; through its parishes, the church could readily mobilize considerable pressure on individual legislators.

However, by 1977 the example of other states altered the situation. Illinois lawyers recognized that their state had fallen far behind the rest of the nation. A number of study efforts emanating from the governor's office, the Chicago Bar Association, and the Illinois State Bar Association culminated at approximately the same time and pointed to no-fault as a desirable divorce policy in order to eliminate the fraud inherent in the bogus grounds cited in most divorces. Several bills were thrown into the legislative hopper; some provided for comprehensive reform of the divorce code following the guidelines of the UMDA; others simply would have added no-fault to the list of grounds upon which a divorce could be obtained.

The chief proponent of the divorce reforms which were finally adopted was not a member of the legislature but a prominent divorce attorney, Marshall Auerbach. He was a partner in a powerful Chicago law firm whose name member was also a commissioner of the NCCUSL. His connections opened important doors, particularly to the Daley machine; eventually they led to co-sponsorship of his bill by Mayor Daley's son, Richard, who himself was a rising politico. Auerbach's bill would change most of Illinois divorce practice but it did not embrace no-fault for divorce itself. A competing bill, sponsored by the Chicago Bar Association and an attorney rival of Auerbach's, would have left much of the divorce code unchanged but it added no-fault to the list of divorce grounds.

Auerbach spent much of his time for several months lobbying for his bill. He succeeded because of his ability to build a coalition of liberals who wanted divorce reform and conservatives who opposed no-fault. Most prominent among the opponents of no-fault was the Illinois Catholic Conference, which sent a letter to each member of the General Assembly just before the crucial vote on no-fault's adoption articulating its opposition to no-fault divorce because it might make divorce easier and therefore destabilize family life. Largely on the basis of that letter, Auerbach's bill passed while the rival bill failed. Thus Illinois removed consideration of fault from all ancillary divorce matters such as alimony, property division, and child custody, but it left fault grounds for the divorce itself.

It took Illinois another six years, when the situation had changed further, before no-fault itself was added as a ground for divorce. By 1983, attorneys had become accustomed to no-fault for property division and custody questions; fault for the divorce itself had become an anomaly. The Catholic church's opposition had also weakened; it was more difficult for it to oppose no-fault on principle because the idea was already so deeply embedded in divorce law. Moreover, with Illinois being one of only two states without no-fault divorce, the pressure on its legislators to catch up was enormous. However, the church did not capitulate without a fight. It had enough power and interest in the issue to cause a delay in legislative consideration. During that delay, the bill's sponsors met with the Illinois Catholic Conference and arranged a compromise. In return for inserting a six-month waiting period for consensual divorces, the conference agreed to remain neutral. With that provision, the bill passed and Illinois became the forty-ninth state to provide no-fault divorce.

As a late adopter, Illinois proceeded very differently from Iowa; the process was also different than in Wisconsin because feminists were not heard during the divorce debates. In Illinois, the attention of feminists was riveted on obtaining ratification of the ERA from the legislature, an effort that ultimately failed but which drained all energy from alternative agendas. However, the Catholic church played a far more visible role than in Iowa (where it is weaker) or Wisconsin. The legal profession and its organizations were influential in formulating the bills but ultimately divided among themselves. That division reflected both differences in principle and personal rivalry.

The debate about no-fault was more visible in Illinois than in most states. The principal newspaper of the state, the *Chicago Tribune*, not only covered the legislative debate as it unfolded but also had an exceptionally large number of feature stories about no-fault divorce and its potential consequences. On the other hand, the coverage was considerably sanitized. Readers of the *Tribune* would assume that the legislative debate was much more thorough and reasoned than in fact it was. For instance, the *Tribune* did not report the debate on 23 June 1977, after which one of the bills was defeated. That debate occupied only eight pages of transcript, three of which were taken up with the introduction of Miss South Dakota and her serenading the assembly. It was neither an enlightened nor intense discussion of the merits of a complex piece of legislation.[56] But despite such shielding of legislative antics, the actions of Illinois legislators on divorce reform were more openly reported than those of most states.

Wisconsin

Wisconsin considered no-fault in the same year as Illinois, but finished the task more rapidly. By 1977 it had a full-fledged no-fault statute which also included important property division provisions.

Wisconsin had a longer tradition of adjusting its divorce code than many states. Rather than leave the divorce provisions of its statutes alone for generations, it had thoroughly revised its divorce laws as recently as 1960, when it adopted a comprehensive system of conciliation together with a prohibition on remarriage within a year of a divorce and the requirement of court permission for parents of dependent children to remarry. Moreover, since as early as 1878, Wisconsin law had permitted divorce when a couple had been living apart for five years, a provision that was eventually recognized as approaching no-fault.[57] In 1969 that period was reduced to one year.[58]

No-fault as the only ground for divorce, however, did not arrive in Wisconsin without considerable open conflict in the mid-1970s.[59] The effort began in 1975, when proponents of no-fault sought to follow the example of most states by proposing a bill which would have simply added no-fault to the existing fault grounds of Wisconsin law; that strategy had aroused little controversy in most states and promised quick success. As in Illinois, church interests opposed the measure, but that opposition was not the principal obstacle faced by the bill. No-fault lost in the Wisconsin Senate when feminist supporters voted against it because they had become concerned with the financial consequences of divorce. This outcome reflected the fact that the Wisconsin legislature had a small but articulate group of feminist supporters who held the balance of power in this vote.

At the next biennial session of the legislature, feminists forced inclusion of their economic concerns in a more comprehensive divorce reform bill. Those feminists had joined together largely as the result of previous contacts with one another through the Wisconsin Governor's Commission on the Status of Women and work on other feminist causes in the legislature. They had become alerted to the economic problems of divorced women at a regional conference of state commissions on the status of women in 1974. Most of the activists lived near Madison, the state capital, and were easily able to communicate with one another.

Thus in Wisconsin, unlike most states, no-fault became linked to changes in property division at divorce through the active intervention of feminist advocates. That enlarged the scope of conflict considerably. No longer was divorce reform an obscure, largely consensual matter, which addressed a technical legal problem with a technical legal solution. Rather, it became an issue which pitted feminists against many lawyers and divided the legal profession because of the uncertain consequences of the property division law. It even set feminists against each other, because some favored equal distribution of marital assets while others wanted to allow judges to exercise discretion while dividing assets according to a standard of equitable distribution. The visibility of the struggle increased considerably.

The Wisconsin effort also involved outsiders to an unusual degree. Herma Hill Kay, who had been both a key author of the California law and co-reporter of the Uniform Marriage and Divorce Act, was a personal acquaintance of one of the

Wisconsin reformers and came several times to Wisconsin to speak about divorce reform.[60] The legislative director of the NCCUSL provided the Wisconsin group an analysis of their proposal in the light of the Uniform Marriage and Divorce Act.[61] Thus both the California experience and the expertise of the NCCUSL played a far more prominent role in Wisconsin than in Iowa or in most of the other states on which we have information.

When Wisconsin passed no-fault in 1977 it was not the inevitable outcome of a routine policy process. No-fault, together with marital property reform, came to Wisconsin as the result of careful planning by feminist advocates, who used the sentiment in favor of no-fault to obtain what they thought would be more favorable financial treatment of wives at the time of divorce, and also as the result of an overt conflict dominated by competing interest groups. By entering an arena previously dominated by attorneys, feminists enlarged the issue. The initial supporters of no-fault were unable to evade feminist concerns as they had avoided Catholic apprehensions in many states. Nor were they able to appease feminists through quiet backstage negotiations.

Conclusion

The march of no-fault divorce through the states utilized an emulation process which capitalized on some of the key characteristics of the no-fault proposals. The general acceptance of the no-fault idea (representative of the time-is-ripe argument) undoubtedly legitimated no-fault in the eyes of many legislators. Its cost-free character made it easier for legislators to accept, especially in an era during which others agitated for tax cuts and reduced state revenues. Policy sponsors lent their skills to the proposals in guiding them successfully through the shoals of the legislative process. Those traits made no-fault an excellent candidate for rapid diffusion. Because it carried no costs and was accompanied by little or no controversy, state legislatures were easily persuaded that they should join the bandwagon. Although no-fault did not bestow any material or competitive advantages to adopting states, its acceptance was a matter of pride in keeping up with modern trends in offering the state's citizens as good a divorce law as other states did. Emulation was particularly easy if the state only needed to add no-fault to existing divorce grounds, even though it made little logical sense to have an appended no-fault ground for divorce since no-fault implied the denial of grounds as prerequisite for getting a divorce. Logic, however, often takes second place to convenience in the legislative process.

We may summarize the routine policy process in the emulation phase with the following characteristics: no cost; frequent resort to the incremental strategy of simply adding no-fault to existing grounds; high perceived legitimacy of no-fault because of its acceptance elsewhere; presentation as a technical solution to a technical legal problem; little public visibility; and narrow interest-group participation. These characteristics occurred frequently.

Yet on several occasions no-fault broke out of the confines of the routine policy mode into a conflictual mode. Emulation is not always blind; the prior acceptance of a new policy by other states is a two-edged sword. In addition to making the policy appear legitimate, it also eventually reveals unanticipated problems and permits groups to attempt to broaden the debate by entering the policy-making arena. That is what occurred in two instances of late adoption of no-fault, the case of the Catholic church in Illinois and of feminists in Wisconsin.

This suggests that at least two emulation processes exist. The first promotes acceptance of the principles underlying the legislation of innovating states even though it does not necessarily lead to exact duplication. It is typified by the routine policy-making process and occurs with minimal conflict, media exposure, group activity, or expert advice. It is a rapid process.

The second occurs later in states that had originally resisted the innovation. It is more conflictual, involves more interest groups, obtains greater media attention, and may be accompanied by an expansion of the issues involved in the legislation. The difference occurs because of two factors. One is that unanticipated defects in the policy become visible after it has been in operation for some years; the late adopters seek to avoid those problems. Secondly, late emulators are at the end of the queue because a variety of social and political forces had led them to resist joining the bandwagon at an earlier time. Thus, promoters of no-fault confronted more hostile conditions in states like Illinois and Wisconsin than in Iowa or Michigan. Those conditions made it less likely that the issue would be addressed by routine policy making.

The manner by which no-fault divorce diffused across the nation is certainly not unique in the annals of state policy making. Mansbridge's description of the travails of the Equal Rights Amendment[62] shows a similar process, with swift, unconsidered approval by the early adopters and severe conflict and ultimate rejection in the states that dealt with it toward the end of its consideration period. On the other hand, no-fault divorce has characteristics that are not shared by many policies considered by the states. Unlike many issues, no-fault divorce was not promoted by federal government incentives. It did not involve public expenditures. It was not generally associated with a social movement that might draw it into broader public controversies, as was the case of abortion legislation.

7

The Transformation of
Property at Divorce

Property and gender lie at the heart of the American social and
economic regime. Since the nation's creation they have determined political as well as economic status. At the outset, those
men who owned property could vote; the remaining free men
were relegated to the periphery of the political arena, while
slaves were not even full-fledged persons because they were
owned by others.[1] Women were excluded from the political
arena because they were women. Although political power has
since been dispersed to all citizens, personal worth in the
United States continues to be commonly measured by the size
of the bank account, the location of the home, the nameplate
on the car, far more than the family name. Obversely, the poor
are shamed by their poverty; when helped, degrading rituals
such as soup lines, background investigations, or special
vouchers accompany the assistance.

Consequently, it is not surprising that many of the most
heated political controversies center around proposals to regulate or deregulate property ownership. Private ownership has
always been considered sacrosanct by the general consensus in
the United States, and every attempt to breach it, whether for
public utilities or parklands, sparks controversy. Almost any
proposal for governmental regulation in the ownership or use
of private property stimulates sharp conflict. For example, proposals for higher taxes meet profound hostility not just because
they take more from private hands, but also because they increase the ability of government to intervene in other ways.
Many oppose antitrust laws and public utility regulation on

grounds that they decrease economic efficiency; likewise, zoning regulations which regulate use of land and buildings are resisted by those who would like to do whatever they please with the property they own.

Married women lacked full rights over property until the middle of the nineteenth century, a disability that symbolized their subordinate status. Even today, the fact that a woman's housekeeping activities go unpaid suggests inferiority, reinforced by the fact that when women enter the labor market, they earn less on the average than men.

Thus it is profoundly puzzling to find that only scattered controversy accompanied the profound changes that culminated in the 1970s in the law governing the power of husband and wife to own, control, and manage property. These changes were accomplished by avoiding the shibboleths of government intervention or economic efficiency. The advocates of such changes managed to channel them in the routine policy-making process, obscuring their effect in the complexity of family property law and justifying them by the gradual character of the proposed changes so that potential opponents were hard pressed to point to a single event or alteration which undermined the old regime.

Marriage and Property

Property has always been a central element of marriage. In many cultures, obtaining a wife required payment to the bride's or groom's family because of the economic implications of shifting the young woman from one family to another.[2] A corollary of such relationships was that a wife was often considered property and was expected to contribute to the husband's welfare through her work and by mothering and raising children. The family was a haven for the wage-earner and a structure for supporting dependent children until they too could contribute to the economy of the family. The value of children was often their potential contribution to the family's welfare.[3] Unless apprenticed to someone else, they were expected to work around the house or beside their father; in their parents' old age, it was presumed that they would provide financial support and a place for the parents to live if needed. For some, families and their property relationships were a means to accumulate capital to improve their long-term economic condition. The investment of long working hours by husband, wife, and children in family enterprises was seen as an avenue for escaping poverty and dependence on employers.

Control over property has often been closely associated with the distribution of power *within* the family. Husbands predominated in the United States. Until the middle of the nineteenth century, marriage deprived a woman of control over all property that she owned beforehand, that was given to her at marriage, or that she might earn during it. The husband could sell, trade, or use these in any manner he wished. A wife needed her husband's permission to take a wage-earning job. Upon his death, she had a claim to the use of one-third of his real property during her life but nothing more unless it was explicitly willed to her. A married woman's legal status contrasted sharply with that of the single woman who never married and could own property in the same way as a man. In a society where ownership of property played a central role in determining status, wives were clearly in an inferior position. A husband's propertied status determined the wife's rather than the reverse: women might marry "up" or "down" and acquire their husband's position, but men, while they might acquire property from a marriage, rarely lost status by marrying a woman from a less wealthy family.

Children were in an even more inferior position. Children could not own or manage property until they reached their legal majority or had left their parents' home. Whatever a minor child earned belonged to the father.

Both wife and children depended upon the man of the house for their livelihood; their standard of living hinged on his tastes. If he wished to live beyond his means and put the family into debt, that was his prerogative. If he insisted on a miserly existence well below his means, that was also his privilege.

The history of family property law in the United States is characterized by the decline of the autocratic power of the husband-father. It is one full of subtle changes but little public controversy. To understand the manner in which its alteration remained within the boundaries of the routine policy process, we need to trace it to its beginnings in the late 1830s.

Nineteenth-Century Marital Property Acts

The law of property governing the wife's disability to own property had been carried to the United States from England together with most other common law. It had medieval origins, both in its religious concept of the merger of a wife into the legal person of her husband, and in its feudal function of making certain that all property was held by a male who could provide military service to his lord. Under the common law, a married woman had no separate legal identity: in addition to not owning property, she was barred from entering into a contract, being sued, or engaging in any other legal action without the consent of her husband. The roots of this legal unity were deep, as Norma Basch explains:

The concept functioned in a diversity of historical contexts. Its religious origins lay in the one-flesh doctrine of Christianity, its empirical roots in the customs of medieval Normandy. Its introduction into English law after the Normal Conquest signaled a decline in the status of English wives which reached a nadir in the early capitalism of the sixteenth and seventeenth centuries. It was part of the baggage that English colonists carried to the New World. But what is most striking about the long course of the concept of marital unity is its ability to serve the legal needs of three shifting social structures: the kin-oriented family of the late Middle Ages, the patriarchal nuclear family of early capitalism, and even the more companionate nuclear family of the late eighteenth century.[4]

However, the common law also had for a long time been modified by arrangements in equity which provided loopholes. Wealthy fathers who did not have faith in their prospective sons-in-law and wished to endow their daughters with an inheritance they could use free from their husbands' control found a way to accomplish that. They established trusts which separated legal ownership from use. A trustee held title to the property and kept it out of the hands of the woman's husband; the woman, however, had use of the property. Through such legal fictions, some women acquired the fruits of property ownership.

These rules and usages produced a maze of fictions which created difficulties in the more commercial environment of nineteenth-century America, in contrast to the feudal society of sixteenth-century England. In a society in which property changed hands frequently, having some property tied up in trusts made it difficult to convey a clear title. Moreover, women who had such trusts borrowed money, but complex rules governed the conditions under which such property could be attached for payment of a delinquent debt and made it perilous for creditors to lend money to married women. Thus, these trusts were one of the many complications that impeded free trade and use of property, and they became a target of new commercial interests in the first third of the nineteenth century.

As Rabkin suggests, the legal reformers of the early nineteenth century aimed at several objectives: defeudalization, commercialization, and simplification of the law.[5] Their tool was codification of the law by the replacement of many judge-made common law rules and equitable principles with legislation modeled after the French civil code. These objectives merged, as Basch shows, with a desire to ease the impact of economic crises upon debtors and to remove the peculiar disabilities that the common law imposed on married women.[6]

One of the first casualties of the assault on the old legal order was the trust instrument as it had been developed for the benefit of married women. In New York, the Revised Statutes adopted in 1836 eliminated most "uses," that is, the practice of one party benefitting from property while someone else, the trustee, held ownership.[7] Consequently, the trust in favor of married women was impaired; since married women were not entitled to hold property on their own, they and their fathers suddenly lost this protective device. No other simple procedure existed to permit a father to endow his daughter with property that would be beyond the grasp of her husband. The reforms made it easier for men to transfer property and for creditors to know what property they could grasp for repayment of debts, since all of a family's property was owned by the husband. For most transactions, the new law was an improvement. Only those relatively few married women who had benefited from marital trusts were now deprived of privileges which they had long enjoyed, and fathers no longer had a device to protect their daughters' fortunes.

The Married Women Property Acts in New York were adopted in part as a response to this situation by giving limited property rights to married women.[8] The 1848 act permitted women to own property they brought into the marriage and property that they inherited. But the law also was a response to the plight of heavily indebted families who found that property brought by wives to the marriage was not protected from the debts incurred by husbands. In addition, the new laws partially met feminist objections to the legal subjugation of women which both male and female advocates of women's rights began to articulate at this time.

While the new law succeeded in protecting a married woman's interest in property by making it unavailable for payment of her husband's debts,[9] it led to new complications which hampered her free use of the property. The new law used the language of equity courts in stating that married women held such property "to their sole and separate use,"[10] a formulation that permitted the New York courts to interpret the new law according to the earlier presumptions of equity courts. In prior cases under equity, those words had meant that if a creditor did not name the exact property which served as guarantee for the loan, he could not collect it; the courts now applied the same rules to the new statute.[11] Thus, commercial transactions involving married women became more complicated rather than simpler, although affluent women did gain some degree of control over their fortunes. The New York legislature attempted to clarify this situation with amended statutes in 1860 and 1862, but it failed to alter the courts' interpretation until new legislation specifically repealed it in 1884.[12]

However, wages were another matter: the 1884 change and the ones preceding it did not suffice to protect a married woman's wages from her husband's control. As late as 1901, a married woman in New York was denied the right to sue for lost wages because of an injury caused by her employer. The New York courts held "at common law the husband was absolutely entitled to the services and earnings of his wife, and neither the enabling act of 1860, nor the broader one of 1884, has affected this right . . ."[13] Only the husband could sue for the lost wages of his wife; it was implicit in this ruling that the wages of a married woman belonged to the husband rather than wife, unless she explicitly directed them to her separate account at the time of her employment. That led to still another statute in 1902, by which the legislature explicitly gave married women the right to control their own earnings.

The struggle to enact rights for married women to control their own property was thus long and complex in New York. It has not been thoroughly documented for other states, but probably often followed parallel paths.[14] In New York it began as part of the codification movement to simplify commerce and to relieve the pressure of indebtedness felt by some families. To these was added the desire of affluent fathers to endow their daughters with independent wealth that could be kept out of the grasping hands of untrustworthy sons-in-law. By the middle years of the century, feminists added their voice against the belittlement symbolized by the legal practice and the real constraints it imposed upon women. However, the extension of the right to own and control property to all married women, particularly those whose only property consisted of their wages, took an additional half century of agitation in New York by both legal simplifiers and advocates of women's rights.

These origins of the Married Women Property Acts explain why they did not arouse a storm of controversy. They were only a small part of the larger movement to simplify and codify the law; they represented a portion of the response to difficult economic times in the late 1840s; and although they had universal application, only a small fraction of all married women were wealthy enough to benefit from their provisions. Revision of married women's property rights aroused some discussion but little open debate in the New York legislature.[15] A few people focused on their potential effect upon spousal relationships, although in practice they had very little impact on the relationship between wives and husbands.[16] As Friedman notes,

... the debates were only modest and fitful. Newspapers made almost no mention of the laws. Little agitation preceded them; great silence followed them. It was the silence of a *fait accompli*.[17]

These laws, their origins, and their social significance were in fact not rediscovered until the mid-twentieth century by legal historians.[18]

Yet the Married Women Property Acts had important symbolic and practical consequences. The symbolic consequence was their lifting of a significant disability from women. Entering marriage no longer carried such a high price for a woman. As feminism became a stronger force in the later years of the nineteenth century, these laws provided support to their assertions of equality.[19]

The practical effects were both direct and subtle. The direct effect was that it provided the means by which women could emancipate themselves to some degree from the whims of their husbands. Divorce was no longer required to enable a married woman to strike out on her own. Because divorce remained stigmatized and difficult to obtain, the Married Women Property Acts provided a small escape hatch from oppressive marriages for some women.

The subtle practical consequence was that these laws created a new category of property. Before they existed, there was only one type of family property: the husband's. After a Married Women Property Act was adopted, a second category appeared: the wife's. All subsequent legal development took that category into account.

Property and Divorce

The Married Women Property Acts were not part of the law of divorce. Divorce law followed a separate path of development which, however, was influenced by the adoption of the Married Women Property Acts.

The financial affairs of divorcing couples were controlled by private agreements which were negotiated in the shadow of a wide variety of legal provisions. We are here following the development of those statutory arrangements, but one should not lose sight of the fact that most divorces were uncontested, the result of negotiated settlements between the two spouses and their attorneys. We know very little about the character of those settlements, but the conventional wisdom is that they did not necessarily mirror the provisions of the statutes. Some were more generous, others more stingy to the wife. Judges routinely approved them without substantial scrutiny. As long as they were not unconscionable, they would usually withstand later attack in court, and, of course, very few of them came back to court regardless of how dissatisfied one or the other ex-spouse became.

Two somewhat different devices existed for disposing of property at the time of a divorce: alimony and property division. In some states the law provided for both; in others, only alimony existed although it served the purpose of property division as well. Fault played a very large role in both.

The historical basis for the two was distinct. Alimony had the function of continuing the husband's obligation to support an innocent wife for the rest of her life or until she remarried and became dependent upon another husband. That lifelong obligation was a remnant of earlier legal provisions which prohibited absolute divorce and only permitted a divorce "from bed and board," the equivalent of what now is termed a separation agreement. Since husband and wife were one, a husband's obligation to support his wife continued when absolute divorce became available, as long as the divorce was not her fault and she did not remarry. These provisions also reflected the economic fact that divorced women would have a difficult time supporting themselves; requiring continued support from their ex-husbands reduced the likelihood that ex-wives would become dependent on public welfare.

Property division often was associated with alimony. Many statutes held that when alimony was insufficient to support the innocent wife, some of the property of the husband could be transferred to the wife. A typical law of this sort was Michigan's statute, which read:

Upon every divorce from the bond of matrimony for any cause except that of adultery committed by the wife . . . if the estate and effects awarded to the wife shall be insufficient for the suitable support and maintenance of herself . . . the court may further decree to her such part of the personal estate of the husband and such alimony out of his estate real and personal to be paid to her in gross or otherwise.[20]

Such statutes required judges to take the financial condition of both into account. If the wife had sufficient property of her own (now that she could own property by herself), no such division would be ordered. However, if the wife had insufficient resources to support herself, a judge could order some of the husband's property to be transferred to the wife.

The property of each was determined principally by an examination of who held title to it. Property in the name of the husband was generally his; that in the name of the wife was hers. Since most property was routinely held in the husband's name, at least in the nineteenth century, most property went to the husband at divorce. Over time, court decisions and statutes began to permit judges to examine how the property was acquired and whether the wife had contributed to it by the investment of her own property or through her labor. The most important test in most states, however, continued to be which person was named in the title as owner. These statutes and court decisions left much to the discretion of the judge. While they attempted to establish general guidelines, neither statutes nor court decisions succeeded in specifying precisely what a wife might expect. It generally depended upon the particular circumstances of the case and the inclinations of the judge.

The rules were different for couples who lived in one of the eight community property states.[21] These states drew much more on the experience of civil code countries of continental Europe than on the English common-law tradition with respect to family property, and utilized three categories of family property. Each spouse might own property; this was property which he or she owned before the marriage or had received as an inheritance and which had not been given to the other spouse as a gift. Thus there was his property and hers. In addition, a third category consisted of property acquired during the marriage. Such "community" property was jointly owned and each spouse had claim to half of it. During a marriage, the husband had control over it and managed it. At divorce, however, half belonged to each spouse regardless of who had been the wage-earner.[22]

In both common-law title states and in community property states, fault was an important element in the disposition of property at divorce. The spouse at fault often was penalized. In California (a community property state), for instance, the "innocent" spouse was eligible for more than half of the community property.[23] In noncommunity property states (the so-called common-law states), if the wife was at fault she often could claim none of her husband's property, nor could she get alimony. Sometimes this penalty was attached only to those wives guilty of adultery; sometimes it was the consequence of any kind of fault.[24]

Considerable confusion existed in the distinction between alimony and property distribution. In those states allowing only one or the other, the criteria for awarding such a payment often seemed inappropriate. For instance, where the statute made no provisions for alimony, the criteria sometimes listed such factors as the ability of the wife to find employment or the length of marriage, norms more appropriate to alimony than to property settlement. On the other hand, where alimony alone was permitted, the statute might list the contribution of each spouse to the property which had been accumulated, a norm appropriate for property distribution but not alimony.[25]

However, the distinction had significant consequences for enforcement of the paying spouse's obligation. If the obligation were a property settlement, it would ordinarily be paid immediately. However, alimony was a continuing obligation of the ex-husband and would require a long series of payments. If those payments ceased prematurely, contempt proceedings would have to be brought. In fact, few wives obtained an alimony award and most ex-husbands who had such an obligation defaulted, and their ex-wives rarely went back to court to attempt to collect it.[26]

This maze of state law slowly changed during the late nineteenth century and the early years of the twentieth. Change came about in two ways: through legislation and through court interpretation of existing law. As Friedman suggests is true of much legal innovation,[27] it began in states on the periphery of legal developments when a novel approach to property division at divorce was adopted by Kansas in 1889 and by Oklahoma in 1893. The Kansas statute presciently provided:

[With regard to] such property, whether real or personal, as shall have been acquired by the parties jointly during their marriage, whether the title thereto be in either or both of said parties, the court shall make such division between the parties respectively as may appear just and reasonable, by a division of the property in kind, or by setting the same apart to one of the parties, and requiring the other thereof to pay such a sum as may be just and proper to effect a fair and just division thereof.[28]

Most of the characteristics of marital property distribution codes adopted in the 1980s exist in these provisions. Oklahoma's 1893 statute incorporated much of the language of the Kansas law, but it was somewhat more restrictive in that only marital property (in the community property sense) was to be distributed.[29] It is unknown how these provisions found their way into Kansas law; they did not, however, begin a stampede toward distribution of marital assets.[30] Rather, the laws of the other states slowly adapted to the changed circumstances of marital property holdings.

The forms taken by the changes were two-fold. One was the quasi-community property route of Kansas and Oklahoma, which made either all property or the property acquired during the marriage available for distribution. The other was to authorize use of the husband's marital property for support of an ex-wife, as in the previously quoted Michigan statute. Moreover, the criteria for division varied from a specific percentage (often one-third) to some version of equitable division, often, as in the Michigan statute, with the use of words like "reasonable," "fair," or "just."[31] None of these changes attracted attention or generated controversy when they were enacted. Thus, in 1981 Cheadle could chide the legal community for missing the transition in most states from common-law title-bound property rules at divorce to quasi-community property rules.[32]

As these changes were being enacted, the social landscape was being transformed. The success of the women's suffrage movement in 1920 gave women not only the vote but also a sense that they were the political equals of men. Although the women's suffrage amendment did not end discrimination against women, it carried a potent symbolic message which began to erode traditional boundaries based on gender alone. Women gradually entered public office; their numbers in the legal profession slowly grew. However, wage discrimination continued and very few married women worked. The presumption was that men should support their wives and children, and to do that they should be enabled to earn a sufficient income. Women's wages were held down both by the norm that only men needed to earn a family wage and because most women worked only until they married.

World War II and the years following changed that entirely. Suddenly millions of women entered the work force, and they remained there. The women who came to work in war industries earned as much as men had because the labor shortages of the war required such pay to recruit them. When the war suddenly ended in August 1945, the norm that only single women should work had been broken. It had become acceptable for women to continue their employment even when they had children. According to Degler, however, married women who worked had a different motivation and purpose than men.[33] Whereas men worked to support their families, women often worked to help their families achieve specific goals, such as a major purchase, putting a child through college, or raising the family's living standard. As Degler put it, while men continued to forge their family life around the requirements of their work, wives adapted their work schedules to accommodate their families.[34] Wives' incomes therefore had the appearance of being supplementary.

As we saw in chapter 2, by the 1970s a majority of wives worked outside the home for pay. They did so to help their families. Thus the division of a family's property into his and hers no longer reflected social reality as well as it had in earlier decades. Many of the goods enjoyed by families and their assets were the product of the paid labor of both spouses, and husbands and wives often considered them to belong to both. Although most were unschooled in law and had never heard the term "marital property," the concept that assets acquired during a marriage belonged to both husband and wife regardless of who happened to hold title was not a revolutionary one in the 1970s.

Reform and the Rise of Marital Property Provisions

When the small band of reformers began to consider no-fault divorce in the 1960s, they confronted these changed social conditions within the context of extraordinary confusion in the law of divorce, especially as it related to the disposition of a couple's property. A multitude of provisions existed in state law about how the assets of a divorcing couple should be handled. Those provisions were located in a variety of places in state codes; they often did not dovetail neatly with each other. They frequently handled distribution of property at death using entirely different legal principles than for the distribution of property at divorce. Still other provisions governed the control of property while a couple was married. Each state seemed to have its own peculiar provisions. The profusion of confusing provisions made it nearly impossible for a lay person to understand the main provisions of these laws. This led Robert Levy to write to his (NCCUSL) committee: "However improbable it might seem to anyone familiar with the need for reforming substantive marriage and divorce doctrines, a persuasive argument can be made that the rules controlling property relationships . . . are in even worse condition."[35]

The NCCUSL effort to create a uniform marriage and divorce act provided the occasion for considering some of these problems. Since fault was closely tied to existing provisions regulating alimony and property division, removing it required an adjustment in the property law as well. However, Levy was very circumspect about how large an effort his committee should make. The problem was enormously complex because ideally it made sense to conform the treatment of family property at divorce with the treatment of family property at a spouse's death and during the marriage. However, another NCCUSL committee was already working on probate law. In addition, revising property relationships during marriage would involve far more controversial matters than just handling divorce because every family would be immediately affected by any change in family property law, whereas only those going through the unanticipated experience of a divorce would be subjected to changes in divorce law.

Even so, more than one-third of Levy's original monograph discussed the intricacies of financial arrangements at divorce. Levy's monograph was an important landmark in the development of new concepts for these arrangements. His eighty-seven–page discussion of financial arrangements buttressed by an equal number of pages listing the provisions of the fifty states were themselves an event. No such listing had existed before Levy's publication, and the only similarly detailed examination of property laws had only just been published by Clark in a family law text.[34] Levy's own text contained a much briefer treatment.

Levy recommended pathbreaking changes.[37] The first was to count the wife's homemaking contribution as equal to her husband's wages. This echoed the recommendation of President Kennedy's Commission on the Status of Women in 1963 which had stated:

Marriage is a partnership to which each spouse makes a different but equally important contribution. This fact has become increasingly recognized in the realities of American family living.[38]

Levy had earlier noted this recommendation in his family law text and now repeated it to the NCCUSL.

Secondly, Levy recommended that fault be eliminated in determining alimony and property division. The purpose of no-fault divorce, he argued, was to remove the need to contrive fraudulent evidence and to remove some of the bitterness of the divorce process by putting aside all arguments about misbehavior. Obviously, those ends could not be achieved if the same fault arguments were allowed to reappear in decisions about property.

Third, Levy recommended that a new category of property which would encompass the couple's joint holdings be established for common-law states. Levy called this category "marital" property. It was the equivalent of the community property in community property states. This property would include all assets acquired during the marriage, regardless of which spouse happened to hold title.

Finally, Levy recommended that marital property be divided by provisions "designed to minimize conflict."[39] In his exposition of the potential alternatives, Levy quoted liberally from the Task Force on Family Law and Policy of the Citizens' Advisory Council on the Status of Women, but did not recommend an equal distribution of marital assets "because the time is not yet ripe."[40]

This set of recommendations had one very important quality. While the entire package would appear radical to some, portions of it were familiar in many states. That was particularly true for the division of property. The eight community property states essentially possessed a marital property rule at divorce. A large number of other states permitted an allowance from the husband's estate in order to supplement an alimony award where it was necessary to do so.[41] Some additional states permitted "adjustments" of property rights, and a handful of common-law states came close to the concept of marital property. In addition to Kansas and Oklahoma, Alaska had such a provision which allowed "for the division between the parties of their joint . . . or . . . separate property . . . in the manner as may be just and without regard to which of the parties is the owner of the property."[42] A few other states permitted division of property without reference to alimony. Consequently, Levy's suggestions were not a radical break from the past but could be presented to the conference as incremental changes to existing legal norms in many states.

Other elements of Levy's proposal were more novel. No state included a provision regarding a wife's homemaking contribution, although several gave credit to a wife's specific work-related contribution to property accumulated during the marriage. Finally, fault was deeply embedded in the statutes, particularly as it related to adultery. Women divorced because of their adulterous behavior could not obtain alimony in most states.

Levy's proposals encountered considerable discussion and opposition within the drafting committee and among its advisors. Some proponents of no-fault divorce like Bernard Hellring feared that these proposals would kill the no-fault idea itself.[43] Others found the marital property concept too novel and confusing; there were indications both from Tennessee and Indiana that the proposals were too radical.[44] On the other hand, Alice Rossi advocated an equal division rule to Levy.[45] However, the specification of the homemaker's contribution for dividing marital property left no trace of discussion.

The proposals were closely debated in the committee and it was sharply divided over them.[46] They also encountered spirited debate before the full conference. The broad application of community property concepts in the form of marital property met particular skepticism, with regard both to their utility and to the likelihood of their adoption by state legislatures. In the end, when the ABA Family Law Section urged revision of these sections,[47] it succeeded in adding a new alternative section for community property states.[48] The common-law version made *all* property available for distribution while the alternative for community property states provided only for division of community property;[49] the common-law version (whether by accident or design)[50] also omitted a provision seeking to protect the custodial parent's continued residence in the family home. Both versions mandated division of property without reference to fault and according to a rule of equitable division. Both specifically authorized the court to take into account the contribution of a spouse as a homemaker in making the property division.

Change in actual state law followed a much more tortuous route. California adopted its no-fault law which incorporated provisions that would be featured by the NCCUSL's Uniform Marriage and Divorce Act (UMDA) even before the NCCUSL acted. Like the UMDA, California's law eliminated the consideration of fault in property division, which had previously permitted the innocent party to receive more than half of the community property. Moreover, as the UMDA did, the California law explicitly permitted alimony to be limited for a specified time period depending on the circumstances of the wife. This was not a recommendation of the governor's commission, and it was a radical break from the law of almost every other state.

There were also important differences between the two. California's new law required an equal division of the community property except when "economic circumstances warranted" rather than the equitable division required by the UMDA.[51] As we demonstrated in Chapter 4, the elimination of fault and the proviso for equal division had been discussed for several years in California. The effort to eliminate fault dated back to the 1964 legislative hearings at which no-fault was first proposed by Kay. Equal division logically followed, since consideration of fault had been the principal reason for unequal division of community property.

In other aspects, the California law appeared more conservative than the UMDA draft. It had no provision for counting the contribution of the homemaker in calculating the division of community property. Nor did it urge judges to consider, among the spouse's economic circumstances (as did the UMDA), "the desirability of awarding the family home or the right to live therein for a reasonable period to the spouse having custody of any children."[52]

The changes to California's property law did not attract much attention during the debates on its new divorce law in 1969, perhaps because the state was already governed by community property rules. No-fault was much more prominent in the debates, as were the proposals for a family court and compulsory counseling discussed in Chapter 4. None of the participants interviewed recalled much controversy over these provisions, and neither did Krom's contemporary account.[53]

Most states did not follow California's lead in linking no-fault divorce with no-fault property division or a reform of property laws. Iowa, for instance, made no changes in its property law when it adopted no-fault divorce in 1970; it did not accept marital property concepts until 1980. Many other states amended the provisions for property division either before or after they adopted no-fault.

Almost no state fully adopted the property provisions of the NCCUSL's Uniform Marriage and Divorce Act. Some provisions won wider acceptance than others; some spawned different responses to the same problems. However, the adoption of the marital property concept clearly gathered momentum after the NCCUSL first suggested it in 1970.[54] Twenty-three states accepted it by statutory action between 1971 and 1982.[55] While we have no direct documentary evidence of a link between the NCCUSL's actions and state adoption of these provisions, it is reasonable to conclude that the model provided by the Uniform Marriage and Divorce Act played a role in the diffusion of these provisions.

However, by 1983 only nineteen states had unequivocally eliminated fault from consideration in property division.[56] These were, for the most part, but not exclusively, the states that had adopted a pure no-fault system of divorce; others, like Missouri, outlawed fault in divorce grounds while retaining it for dividing property. Many of the states which had simply added no-fault as an alternative ground for divorce retained consideration of fault with regard to property distribution; eleven states had laws which clearly followed this route.[57] The remainder had statutes that were shrouded in ambiguity.

Equal-distribution criteria also fared poorly, as most states preferred equitable distribution norms which had already been common before the UMDA added its endorsement of them. Only five states, three of which had community property rules, adopted provisions which required equal distribution;[58] another five had ambiguous provisions.[59] The remainder required equitable distribution.

Many state laws began to appear with the long list of considerations included in the UMDA for determining fairness in distribution.[60] The UMDA's list itself resembled the conditions previously mentioned in court cases. The principal addition to the previously court-mandated criteria which may be attributed to the influence of the UMDA model was the homemaking contribution of a spouse. Twenty-two states included such a provision in 1983;[61] none had it in their statutes in 1968. In addition, however, six states[62] went beyond the UMDA by providing that the spouse with custody of the children shall have a special claim to the family home.

Finally, the clear distinction between maintenance (alimony) and property division that the UMDA sought to establish continued to elude some state legislatures. However, many states transformed alimony into a transitional payment in accordance with the UMDA model.[63] Thus alimony was to last only for the time that it was reasonable to expect it would take for the wife to become financially independent, rather than until she died or remarried.

The political process producing these changes in the law of property at divorce did not follow any uniform pattern. In most states the adoption process was as muffled as with the changes in the grounds for divorce. In many states it was even more obscure, since one of the principal players in the no-fault change, the Catholic church, was not aroused by proposed changes in property law. On the other hand, women's and feminist groups in some states engaged in far more open lobbying for property law change than they had when no-fault alone was considered. In every case, matrimonial lawyers played an active role.

These processes are exemplified by California, Wisconsin, Illinois and New York. The stories for the first three are those we have already told in Chapters 4 and 6. As we saw there, little of the general public became involved in the debate. In California, the principal changes in the new law were the elimination of fault, the stricter standard of equal division, and the transformation of alimony to a transitional payment. Although these provisions attracted some notice, they were accepted as part of the general package of reform by the legislative majority which adopted no-fault divorce. California legislators expressed much more concern with the proposals to establish a whole new tier of courts and to require marriage counseling, both of which would have added large expenses to public budgets. In Illinois, no-fault divorce also acted as the lightning rod for whatever controversy occurred. As we have shown in Chapter 6, when the Catholic church expressed its opposition to no-fault divorce, legislators agreed to approve a bill which contained everything but no-fault divorce. That meant that Illinois eliminated fault from property division and accepted the marital property concept with the equitable division norm, including acceptance of the homemaker's contribution. Debate in the legislature did not focus much on those provisions, and neither feminists nor the church expressed interest in the debate. Matrimonial lawyers thoroughly dominated the discussions.

However, as we saw in chapter 6, property provisions attracted considerable attention in Wisconsin. That was the work of feminist legislators and their supporters, who saw an opportunity to improve the condition of women by pushing for the adoption of a marital property provision.[64] As elsewhere, however, feminists were bitterly divided over the appropriate norm to govern distribution. The advocates of equitable distribution won the day in Wisconsin. Feminist advocates remained silent in both California and Illinois, but with split results: in California, as we have noted, the legislature adopted the norm of equal distribution; in Illinois it accepted the equitable standard.

Three years after Wisconsin and Illinois had acted, the same debate occurred in New York but with more visibility.[65] New York still possessed a clearly articulated title property system with no fuzzy edges that might give the wife a claim to her husband's property, even if it had been accumulated during the marriage and even if the wife had been a supportive homemaker. In New York, women who eschewed the feminist label, most notably Julia Perles,[66] had long been working to change the law under the auspices of a variety of bar groups. As early as 1972, as chairman of an extensive set of hearings of a joint committee of New York's two largest bar associations, Perles explored the possibility of introducing the marital property concept to New York, but the effort failed. A better opportunity to push for a thorough revision of the divorce property division arose in 1979, when the Supreme Court ruled that the Georgia alimony statute was unconstitutional because it provided alimony only for women; the Constitution, the court ruled, required gender-neutral provisions.[67] As in many states, this decision sparked a review of the family law code and particularly the provisions for alimony and property division in New York. The advocates of more liberal property division rules won to their cause some of the leading liberal male legislators in both parties, who by the last years of the 1970s had gained important positions in the state legislature. At the same time, the NOW chapter in New York, one of the most politically active in the nation,[68] supported more radical changes. The result was a fierce legislative battle to change the law, with a substantial portion of the bar in opposition. Women in the legislature were deeply divided over whether to accept equitable distribution, as suggested by the New York County Women's Bar Association under the leadership of Perles, or equal distribution as proposed by NOW. In the end the advocates of equitable distribution prevailed, but at the cost of alienating the more radical feminists in the movement. As with the earlier change in New York's divorce law, the issue crossed party lines, with both Republicans and Democrats among the leading supporters and opponents. However, the Catholic church was entirely silent during the debate. Thus, as in 1966 when New York was the last state to broaden its divorce grounds, it was one of the last to accept the major principles espoused by the UMDA, including the broadening of the pool of property to be distributed, the acceptance of equitable distribution, the elimination of fault, and the specification of the homemaker's contribution as a consideration in the division.

More typical was the adoption of such provisions in Maryland after recommendations by a special governor's commission. The Maryland statute was apparently almost entirely the work of lawyers, with little input by other interest groups. It was adopted during the last days of the 1978 legislative session in the rush that is typical of many state legislative sessions. It attracted little public notice and generated no general debate.[69]

Conclusion

It might be argued that family property law did not really experience a radical change in the 1970s; the changes that occurred were only marginal accretions to existing law. That quality was essential to the easy adoption of the new laws, but it misjudges their effect. As a consequence of these changes, most of the United States had by the mid-1980s adopted a community property rule for divorcing couples. The wife's contribution to the family economy through her homemaking activities was specifically acknowledged in many states. Alimony had been transformed from a permanent obligation to support an innocent ex-wife (until another man accepted the responsibility) to a temporary, transitional payment until the former wife could earn her own living. And in many states fault was outlawed from property division as well as from divorce, with the effect that a "guilty" spouse was not punished and an "innocent" spouse was not rewarded in the distribution of the family's property or in the award of alimony.

Supporters of these changes avoided controversy and conflict by linking the changes to existing practices. In most states, the reforms were not proposed as a grand, comprehensive scheme which might have alerted potential opponents and aroused opposition. Rather, they were presented as narrow, technical proposals by experts in family law. Like no-fault, they involved no public expense, and their private consequences did not appear burdensome to private groups. While it was difficult to estimate how they might affect the distribution of family assets and the support of divorced women, the claim could easily be made that the effects would not be drastically different from the status quo.

In most states, no dramatic disputes highlighting the legislative consideration of these changes attracted media attention. The proposed changes in family property law exhibited a daunting complexity that made them unattractive for media coverage. Consequently, it is not surprising that the consideration of these changes enjoyed limited public visibility. The NCCUSL, as we have already indicated in chapter 5, did not attract media attention even though it debated these changes extensively. Perhaps the most revealing discussions took place in the drafting committee's deliberations, for we know that Levy raised many fundamental social issues about the economic condition of divorced women and of children of divorce in his monograph. Unfortunately, transcripts of those deliberations are not available, and the echoes of the committee's debates did not reach state capitols when legislatures considered comparable proposals. Instead, they were often adopted with little public attention.

8

What Should Happen to the Children?

The third major element of divorce law concerns children. Many divorcing couples have minor children whose care needs to be restructured. With father and mother going their separate ways, provision must be made for the care and support of children. Fundamental changes in that aspect of the law also occurred during the late 1970s and early 1980s.

The law's treatment of children has gone through four phases in the United States. Until the middle of the nineteenth century, children were considered the father's asset and responsibility. From approximately the 1850s to the 1940s, as fathers increasingly worked outside the home, children were presumed to belong in their mother's custody because maternal care was considered to be best for the child. Over the course of the twentieth century, judges' decisions subtly shifted the emphasis from maternal preference to the "best interest of the child," which, however, generally continued in practice to mean maternal custody. Finally, by the middle 1970s, state law increasingly emphasized gender neutrality and began to look with favor upon joint custody by both parents.

These shifts followed parallel changes in how Americans viewed the roles of parents and the value of children. In the early years of the nation, when it was still predominantly agricultural, children were important members of the family labor force. They worked with their parents from an early age. Even in towns and cities, children began working during their youth and contributed to the family income. When a family broke apart, it was usually because one or both parents died.

Divorce was an infrequent occurrence and child custody was not an issue requiring much public attention. It seems likely that most of the rare divorces led to informal arrangements for the children, who were probably placed with whatever relative could afford to keep them. However, the law carried over England's common-law preference for fathers, who could best provide for their children.[1] In an 1836 New York case, the judge wrote: "In this country, the hopes of the child in respect to its education and future advancement is mainly dependent on the father."[2] A few years later, another New York judge noted that the father "had better title to the custody of their children" than the mother.[3]

The father's predominant rights, however, were not universally accepted and did not long survive.[4] By the late 1840s, many courts were seizing discretion for themselves and making decisions based on the judge's perception of the interests of the child. And whereas in earlier years judges gave considerable weight to the father's better ability to provide financial resources and pass on an inheritance, mid-nineteenth-century courts considered the mother's ability to nurture more important. This was a reflection of the emergence of the idealized nuclear family, in which wives were consigned to motherhood while men were expected to earn their family's livelihood. The "Cult of True Womanhood" ascribed to mothers the ideals of piety, purity, submissiveness, and domesticity;[5] motherhood was a woman's ultimate accomplishment. It was thought that children were best cared for by mothers, who could shield them from immoral influences. The law reflected these sentiments in its articulation of the "tender years doctrine," which developed in some places through legislation and in others through judicial opinion. At the beginning sons and daughters were treated differently, with fathers having a larger claim upon sons who might be ready to enter the work force while daughters were always thought to be better off in the households of their mothers.[6] By the last decades of the century, however, all dependent children were thought better off with their mothers. Women were expected to spend most of their lives raising their children, a task for which they were deemed better suited than their husbands.

Although nineteenth-century feminists objected to the consignment of women to the hearth, these role characterizations were not the object of great public controversy because they reflected dominant social values. Consequently, it seemed natural for legislators to write into their state codes and for judges to endorse the norm that mothers should be given custody of children, especially if they were in their "tender" years. The tender years doctrine became an almost universal standard for deciding child custody in divorce. From the late nineteenth century onward, both popular and legal norms dictated that, except in unusual circumstances, children belonged with the mother. A father gained custody only when the mother was demonstrably incapable of performing her duties, either because of mental illness or because of moral perversion. Some judges extolled the virtues of motherhood in superlatives, like the Wisconsin judge who wrote:

For a boy of such tender years nothing can be an adequate substitute for mother love—for that constant ministration required during the period of nurture that only a mother can give because in her alone is duty swallowed up in desire; in her alone is service expressed in terms of love.[7]

The father's better capacity to provide for his children was no longer considered. Even the children's wishes were not necessarily consulted, although as they grew older they perhaps had a greater voice in the decision.[8]

Child custody in divorce was not a concern for most social reformers, because divorce continued to be an exceptional occurrence and relatively few children were separated from one parent or the other as its consequence. Instead, social reformers and legislators of the Progressive Era focused their attention on children who seemed much more vulnerable—orphans and "wayward" immigrant children. Those concerns led to the establishment of large new institutions for children: orphanages to care for the homeless and reformatories for those involved in petty crimes or considered to be unmanageable at home or in school.[9] In addition, public schools in the large cities swollen with immigrants were given the task of keeping children out of mischief and indoctrinating them in the ways of American life. Through these developments a public law of child welfare became imposed on the poor that brushed only lightly upon intact, mainstream families. These latter were governed by a private family law which less frequently was the object of legislation, but developed instead through private agreements and the decisions of courts in individual divorce cases.

At the same time as custody presumptions shifted from father to mother, the value of children changed.[10] Children were being forced out of the labor market by legislation which severely limited the hours they could work and the jobs they could take and which required that they attend school for most of their growing years. Those developments sharply altered the economic value of children. Instead of being contributors to the economic well-being of their families, they became financial burdens. However, their value was not simply deflated. Rather, its basis shifted from predominantly economic considerations to largely psychological ones. Children came increasingly to be valued for the companionship they offered while they were young and when parents aged. As Zelizer shows, an even higher value was placed on children because of their companionate value than when they had been economic contributors to their families.[11] As that shift occurred, fathers more often felt deprived when custody was automatically given to their estranged wives. Their psychological deprivation sometimes outweighed the economic benefit from not having custody.

By the middle third of the twentieth century, as divorce became more common, judges transformed the tender years doctrine in a subtle way. Less reference was being made to the mother's "natural" superiority in caring for children and more discretion was given to judges by emphasizing "the best interests of the child" ingredient of the child custody standard. In some instances the "best interests of the child" was offered as an alternative to the tender years doctrine, whereas in reality it was simply an elaboration of it. As originally articulated, the tender years doctrine did not give mothers title to children; it placed the children in maternal custody because that was what seemed best for their care. However, there was a mechanistic element to the tender years doctrine; it did not permit much discretion for judges to deviate from maternal custody. The newer emphasis on the "best interests of the child" greatly expanded judges' discretion in custody cases. Their preference for such flexibility reflected the large number of cases when the courts felt compelled to consider more than the gender of the petitioner, because both father and mother seemed equally well (or badly) qualified to care for their children. While in most instances the child's best interest was still presumed to lie in maternal custody, other factors could also be considered, such as the preference of the child if it was old enough to state a mature preference, the health and economic circumstances of the parents, the relationship between parent and child, the child's adjustment to school and community, the stability of the existing or proposed family, and the moral standards of the proposed custodian.[12] Thus the principal change accomplished by the new standard was increased flexibility, which made it easier to justify private arrangements where children (usually in their teens) remained with their father and gave more power to judges when settling custody disputes. In practice the new standard made little difference, because most custody decisions continued to be made by agreement, and most reflected the lingering popular norm that children (especially if they were young) belonged with their mother. However, in litigated cases the best-interest formula allowed somewhat more frequent assignment of custody to fathers.

By the 1970s social norms were once again changing. The presumed superiority of mothers in raising children came under fire from several quarters. Judges noted that as mothers increasingly took jobs and became significant contributors to their family's income, they were less at home to care for their children. Many youngsters became latchkey children, returning after school to empty homes even when the mother was neither head of her family nor its principal wage-earner. In addition, the new feminist movement challenged the presumption that only women could do housework and rear children. It called on men to contribute to household work, and an increasing number of fathers consequently began to take a more active role at home. Fathering came more into vogue. Moreover, divorce was in the course of shifting from an exceptional event to an expected incidence of childhood; with almost half of all marriages ending in divorce, more than a third of all children could expect to live in a divorced family before reaching

adulthood.[13] Thus, removing the father from a child's life had
two consequences which took on added significance with the
prevalence of divorce. One was that a very large number of
children would grow up without knowing their fathers for
much of their childhood, because more than half of all fathers
of divorced children almost never saw their children.[14] The
other was that fathers by the thousands, feeling deprived of the
companionship of their children, might refuse to pay child support. When relatively few families with children were being
divorced, that refusal was more a personal tragedy than a social problem. With divorce becoming the norm, the failure of
fathers to pay created a national scandal.

Consequently, the collection of child support payments became a target of legislation; but unlike other areas of divorce
law, it spilled over to the national arena because of the connection between child support and the federal program providing
aid to families with dependent children (AFDC). The initial
federal thrust in this field was a 1950 amendment to the Social
Security Act known as NOLEO (Notice to Law Enforcement
Officials) which was intended to facilitate the welfare agencies'
collection of delinquent support payments from fathers. Congressional interest broadened with the establishment in 1974
of a parent locator service for finding fathers who were delinquent in their child support payments and whose children were
relying on AFDC,[15] and with other means of fostering more
efficient means of collecting child support payments. By 1984,
Congress mandated withholding funds from delinquent fathers' paychecks and income tax refunds to force payment of
child support; the measure applied to all delinquent fathers,
not only to fathers of children on welfare.[16] In addition, the
law required states to set standardized levels of child support
which would be applied uniformly throughout their jurisdiction.

Thus, at the same time that no-fault divorce came onto the
agenda and many states were revising their property and alimony statutes, child support and custody also came on the
table. The NCCUSL, however, did not recommend drastic
changes from existing practice except with regard to fault.
Whereas many states permitted courts to consider the marital

misconduct of a parent in determining custody, the Uniform Marriage and Divorce Act (UMDA) proposed that "the court shall not consider conduct of a proposed custodian that does not affect his [*sic*] relationship to the child."[17] This proposal was, of course, entirely consistent with the remainder of the document in its effort to eliminate marital fault from divorce proceedings.

Robert Levy had proposed more fundamental changes. In order to reduce court custody fights, he had proposed to the drafting committee a presumption "that the mother is the appropriate custodian—at least for young children, and probably for children of any age."[18] In Levy's opinion, "the Act should discourage those few husbands who might wish to contest" custody by establishing such a presumption.[19] Moreover, Levy recommended a rule that custody decisions could not be overturned, except in extraordinary circumstances, for two years, and that even then the presumption should favor the original custodian.[20]

Levy recognized that his recommendations ran counter to emerging legislative trends in the states and they were not entirely accepted by the conference. Contrary to Levy's recommendation, it retained the "best interest of the child" standard together with a list of criteria for applying it culled from state law and court opinions.[21] However, the conference accepted Levy's two-year embargo on modifications of custodial orders as well as his presumption in favor of the original custodian.[22]

The recommendations in the UMDA were influential in some states' decisions to eliminate fault in custody proceedings, but they were not the predominant thrust which state legislatures chose in the 1970s for handling custody disputes. Their principal efforts to change the law focused on joint custody, a concept not considered by the NCCUSL. Unlike no-fault and marital property, this was a change that did not mirror existing practice. It was an invention that went counter to prevailing assumptions about proper child custody decisions. Unlike no-fault, it was not conceived in response to technical problems in the legal system and it was not a product of legal experts. Rather, it reflected the changing life-styles of middle-class American families and a nascent demand by fathers for greater consideration. It ran counter to the prevailing theories of child welfare held by the mental health community, but those theories proved to be surprisingly vulnerable.

The dominant view of mental health professionals regarding optimal custody arrangements was expressed by three authors (including Sigmund Freud's daughter) representing the fields of law and psychiatry. In a book entitled *Beyond the Best Interests of the Child,* they argued that stability in a child's early relationships was the most important factor in child placement decisions. Therefore, they urged that only one parent should have custody and that the custodial parent could (at his or her discretion) bar the other parent from having contact with the child lest it become confused. The authors also argued strongly against changing custodial arrangements once they had been established. Their argument was boldly stated:

Psychoanalytic theory . . . establishes . . . the need of every child for unbroken continuity of affectionate and stimulating relationships with an adult. That knowledge . . . calls into question those custody decisions which split a child's placement between two parents or which provide the noncustodial parent with the right to visit or to force the child to visit.[23]

The Goldstein, Freud, and Solnit book won wide attention and was often cited in court decisions. It also provoked a spirited opposition which expressed itself in the development of the alternative option of joint custody.

One of the most vigorous early critics was an anthropologist, Carol Stack, who wrote with the knowledge of cultures which did not restrict children to a single parent or set of parents.[24] Stack shifted the argument from a single-minded focus on what might be best for the child alone to a consideration of conditions which might promote greater harmony between divorced parents. She regarded the Goldstein, Freud, and Solnit criteria as an invitation to battle, whereas joint custodial arrangements might encourage cooperative parenting. In advocating joint custody, Stack found herself at the forefront of a new standard.

Indeed, as Stack was writing her critique, a few couples were encouraging courts to experiment with joint custody decrees. Traditionally courts had been wary of approving such arrangements because custody provisions of divorce codes generally provided for custody to be granted to one parent alone. A handful of couples not only litigated the issue successfully but won considerable publicity for their innovation.[25] The mid-1970s cases which were reported in the media were surely not the first instances of joint custody in the nation, but they gave currency to the idea and sparked a wave of legislation. An early compilation of joint custody statutes found only one law, a 1967 statute in North Carolina predating this spate of publicity; the twenty-three others all were adopted between 1977 and 1982.[26]

The spread of joint custody is remarkable because it was practically nonexistent before 1975. Except for the North Carolina statute, which was as much directed to instances of the placement of children in abuse and neglect situations as in divorce, no state explicitly authorized it. Indeed, many courts appeared to be hostile to the idea because the bouncing back and forth between parents that many judges associated with joint custody implied instability in the child's environment. The first accounts of joint custody did not appear in legal periodicals but in the popular press, with accounts of such an arrangement in New York carried by the *Christian Science Monitor*,[27] the Madison, Wisconsin, *Capitol Times*,[28] the *New York Times*,[29] and *Newsweek*.[30] These reports told of pioneering parents who had convinced a judge that joint custody was workable and desirable for their children. However, lawyers and judges alike continued to voice much skepticism. That was reflected in the following account published in the most influential popular book about joint custody:

. . . the judge . . . suddenly turned to me.

"Why do you want to spend so much time with your children?"

"Because I love them. Because I want to be a continuing part of their lives."

"You know, my father never had much time for me," he observed. "When he came home at night, he just read the paper. He was tired." His implication was that he had grown up successfully without a deep time involvement with his father.

"But, your honor," I said, "that was fifty years ago. Times change . . ."

"That what's wrong with all you young people. You always think things change. They don't. . . . It's not in the best interests of the children," he said, "*to bounce them back and forth between their parents* [emphasis in original]. They need a place they can call home. They need their own bed at night."³¹

Most of the stories of joint custody emphasized these points: the opposition of the established legal order and the desire of fathers to have a larger voice in the lives of their young children despite their divorce. It was summarized best by Roman and Haddad's 1978 book, which became the counterpoint to Goldstein, Freud, and Solnit. It was motivated by the personal experience of one of the co-authors, who also happened to be a clinical psychologist. The table of contents summarizes their argument well: the impact of divorce on families; fathers and fathering; ergo, joint custody; joint custody families. Most significant is the shift from the presumption that only mothers can nurture to a recognition that fathers want to have a voice in child care, coupled with the assertion of their abilities to become involved. Roman and Haddad's book was not cited as often by courts as Goldstein, Freud, and Solnit,³² but it was a powerful stimulant to discussion of joint custody in legal journals and to legislative action. In their last chapter they urge legislative action, a call taken up by a large number of fathers' groups across the country who began to draft joint custody bills and seek their introduction and adoption in state legislatures.

Joint custody, more than no-fault or marital property, had the potential for becoming as explosive a public issue as abortion. It touched a raw nerve for both mothers and fathers. For many mothers, the threat of losing sole control over their children struck at the core of their self-identities and feelings of worth. To lose their children, even intermittently, meant to lose the center of their lives. Such women might have opposed joint custody, like those women who opposed abortion because it undermined their identities as women and mothers.³³ They did not do so on an organized basis in the early 1980s because many feminists, such as those belonging to the National Organization for Women (NOW), generally favored the respite that joint custody promised them. On the other hand, conservative women, such as those supporting Phyllis

Schlafly's campaign against abortion, were loathe to oppose fatherhood.

An increasing number of fathers also had developed an emotional investment in their children. As the rhetoric of the feminist movement urged men to take fatherhood seriously, men's groups counseled fathers to seek legal affirmation of their rights after divorce through joint custody arrangements. Men's groups, however, carefully kept the issue narrowly defined as favoring fatherhood. One of their principal spokesmen, in fact, acknowledged that keeping a low profile was a conscious strategy in order to minimize potential opposition.[34]

The potential for social conflict, therefore, was never realized. Legislatures considered joint custody in the same low-keyed manner as the other new divorce rules. No one capitalized on the emotional divisiveness of the proposals and the general public was never engaged in the debate. Legislative deliberations centered around the need to legitimize private agreements which were using joint custody, and they focused on children's need for their fathers. Foes of joint custody were pushed into a posture of opposing fatherhood in legislative bodies dominated by men who were themselves fathers.

Joint custody became a cause around which men's groups and fathers' groups rallied. Such groups had existed since at least the mid-1960s, when several of them appeared before the California legislature's interim committee examining divorce law to complain about alimony and miscellaneous perceived injustices of divorce proceedings. At that time they were very hostile to judges and proposed eliminating adversarial proceedings in divorce.[35] They did not yet advocate joint custody but were already arguing for much stronger visitation rights. In the words of its representative,

. . . this is a two-headed coin. In return for these [i.e., child support] payments, we believe also that a father has the inalienable right to share in his children's upbringing, to experience the pleasure and happiness of watching them grow up.[36]

A similar group also lobbied in Minnesota in the late 1960s, and Robert Levy was aware of their efforts.[37] By the early 1980s, some of the same activists appeared under the banner of various groups to lobby for joint custody in California and

Louisiana, among other states; in some instances they used the name of the Joint Custody Association, in others Equal Rights for Fathers.[38] Elsewhere, similar groups operated under still different names, such as the Committee for Fair Divorce and Alimony Laws that demonstrated before the alimony jail in New York in January, 1973,[39] or Fathers for Equal Rights.[40]

Fathers' groups appear to have been active in many states; of twenty-six surveyed,[41] informants identified fathers' groups as active in fourteen, and in two others they indicated that individual divorced fathers lobbied for a joint custody law.[42] Their efforts, however, were not centrally directed; at best the groups were loosely connected to one another. Many were no more than letterhead groups with little or no institutional structure.[43] None had an organizational infrastructure comparable to NOW's; rather, they were more like the many local feminist groups that Freeman describes as proliferating in the 1970s.[44] The various fathers' groups emanating from the Los Angeles area appear to have been the best financed and sent their newsletters and informational packets to many legislators across the country. They sometimes drafted legislation[45] and often appeared before legislative hearings or sent constituent letters to key legislators. They clearly constituted a major force behind the quick diffusion of joint custody legislation in the late 1970s and early 1980s.

In contrast, feminist organizations were relatively quiescent.[46] In part that was the result of their focus on other issues. For instance, when joint custody legislation was first considered in most legislatures, NOW was still concentrating on obtaining ratification of the Equal Rights Amendment. To some degree, their inattentiveness to joint custody legislation resulted from their inability to monitor continuously the activities of state legislatures; the largest of the feminist organizations, NOW, was much more oriented toward Washington than toward state capitols. Most important, perhaps, was the ambivalence many feminists felt toward joint custody.[47] One feminist objective was to promote shared parenting with fathers so that wives would be emancipated from sole responsibility for the drudgery of housework and could enter the labor market on a more equal footing. That led them to advocate the elimination of gender from custody laws. Yet with both parents equally eligible for child custody and support, some feminists feared that joint custody would be a tool to reduce child support payments which many women desperately needed both for their children and for themselves.[48] These crosscurrents led to spasmodic participation by women and feminists in the debates over child custody. Women legislators sponsored many of the statutes because child custody was considered a woman's issue by male legislators. On the other hand, feminist organizations occasionally appeared in opposition to the bills and sometimes were successful in obtaining revisions that made the laws less threatening to divorcing mothers.

In most states, however, child custody legislation followed the routine policy-making path. When asked to compare child custody legislation with other issues during the same session, informants in the mailed survey generally ranked it among the least controversial items, and in many states it passed by overwhelming margins.

Unlike no-fault, joint custody was not the product of an organization like the NCCUSL, and unlike marital property rules, it was not the result of a long line of judicial interpretations. While new, it was not a radically novel family form and therefore was compatible with existing practices. Indeed, it promised to bring fathering back into children's lives after divorce. The new legislation was rarely the fruit of long study by the legislature or any other governmental body. Rather, it was introduced by legislators who found the idea attractive but who had given it little prior study. It then received a variable degree of scrutiny by legislative committees and in general debate. The range of legislative involvement is well illustrated by the experiences of California, Louisiana, and Illinois.

The California experience portrays the fluidity which marked consideration of joint custody. California, which adopted its first joint custody law in 1979, was one of the earliest states to consider and adopt a joint custody statute. Legislative discussion centered on several issues which were raised by both individuals and groups;[49] the bills were amended in significant ways by committee and on the floor. Yet these maneuvers took place in a low-visibility setting marked by little conflict.

The least controversial segment of the bills was the simple

affirmation that custody could be granted to either or both parents, thus providing the backing of the legislature for what had already become practice in a few voluntary agreements. Such a provision had been introduced in 1976 at the very beginning of the joint custody movement but failed. In 1979 this feature of the proposal attracted almost no debate.

How much weight or preference was to be given to joint custody as compared to sole custody was much more controversial. The state senate bill in 1979[50] made joint custody the presumptive preference only when parents concurred, had a written plan to implement it, and agreed to remain in California. As the bill moved through the legislative process, some legislators also proposed that a child's concurrence should be required. A competing bill originating in the lower house of the California legislature, however, balanced these interests differently. Sponsored by a fathers' group, it gave first preference to joint custody, permitting sole custody only "if a preponderance of the evidence establishes that it is in the best interest of the child that custody should be awarded to one parent or if the parents agree that one parent shall assume custody."[51] The state assembly overwhelmingly passed this bill, but when it went to the senate, it was amended to conform to the earlier bill which gave a preference to joint custody only when parents agreed to it. In addition, the senate accepted what became known as the "friendly parent" amendment,[52] which stipulated that if sole custody were granted, the court would be required to give preference to the parent who is "more likely to allow the child or children frequent and continuing contact with the noncustodial parent."[53] Thus, California got a statute which recognized joint custody, gave it preference when parents agreed upon it, and told judges when sole custody was to be granted to prefer the parent most likely to grant generous visitation to the noncustodial parent.

The California legislature devoted considerable attention to the distinction between physical and legal joint custody. The former meant the physical presence of the children in the households of their custodians and required a periodic shift in residence from one parent's home to the other's. Joint legal custody simply denoted shared decision making about important issues in the child's life, such as medical care, education, and travel; it could be part of a sole physical custody arrangement.

Several features of this legislative process were notable. Fathers' groups played a prominent role in the formulation of at least one of the bills. However, the amendment to prefer the parent most congenial to generous visitation in sole custody situations originated from a woman who was a private citizen and it then was embraced by fathers' groups.[54] On the other side, both individual women with professional interests in custody law[55] and women's groups like the Women Lawyers' Association of Los Angeles,[56] while agreeing to voluntary joint custody, opposed the bill sponsored by men's groups which would have made joint custody presumptively preferred. Established feminist groups played little role in the debate. Moreover, legislative consideration of the bill appeared to provoke little press coverage in California newspapers.

The legislative process seems confused to the outsider with its serial consideration of several bills on the same subject. However, that is not atypical for state legislatures. The last bill passed and signed by the governor controls; until the last bill on the subject was disposed of by the legislature, the outcome remained uncertain. While most of the distinctive features of the fathers' groups bill were amended away before it was passed, the preference for the parent most likely to give generous visitation under sole custody remained. That provision was a new invention and met many of the concerns of the men's groups. Thus the extended debate permitted by the iterative nature of the legislative process provided fathers' groups with several opportunities to press their case and eventually won for them a large portion of their agenda.

Finally, while committees held hearings and legislators spent considerable time on the floor discussing the bill, legislators were not guided by empirical evidence about the potential effects of alternative custody provisions on the welfare of children. Almost no such evidence existed. Consequently, anecdotes from the personal and professional experiences of the legislators dominated the debates, and the discussion centered on the presumed desirability of children having contact with both parents and particularly with fathers, as well as the desire to reduce prolonged conflict between parents. So framed, it was difficult for legislators to oppose joint custody, and few did. But it also meant that experts played a much smaller role in the joint custody debates than in deliberations over marital property or no-fault divorce.

California's acceptance of joint custody was an important landmark because other states took their cue from the state's action; for instance, a number of other states copied its "friendly parent" provision. A survey of legislative leaders indicated that at least six (Connecticut, Idaho, Louisiana, Montana, Nevada, and Ohio) were substantially influenced by California's decision. However, even in those states, legislative leaders were coy about following California's example blindly or too closely. For instance, one Louisiana supporter of a joint custody bill remarked at a committee hearing, "I generally am distrusting of things that come this way from California."[57]

In Louisiana, adoption of joint custody required two legislative sessions as it had in California. In the first, the legislature accepted a bill in 1982 which permitted joint custody when it was deemed to be in the best interest of the child.[58] The following year, the legislature adopted a broader statute[59] which made joint custody the preferred plan and created a rebuttable presumption that it was in the best interests of the child. However, parents were permitted to agree upon sole custody. In contested cases, if sole custody was to be ordered, the parent more likely to allow generous visitation to the other would be preferred. In addition, the statute explicitly rejected a preference based on gender and required that the parent requesting sole custody bear the burden of proof that sole custody was in the best interests of the child. Further clarifying amendments were adopted in the next two legislative sessions, indicating how unsettled the law of custody had become for Louisiana by these changes.

As in California, fathers' groups were the driving force for these changes. The California fathers' group, under the guise of the Joint Custody Association, testified in Louisiana and provided Louisiana officials with a bibliography which listed the handful of studies which had some relevance to the question; one of the Louisiana leaders credited the group with ten years of research on the question, a clear exaggeration of the record which the Joint Custody Association itself had compiled.

There was also a Louisiana group, "Concerned Parents for Children's Rights," which supported the bill. Little opposition surfaced. The 1982 bill was co-sponsored by thirty house members, and passed 97–3 in the House and 30–5 in the Senate.[60]

The casual character of legislative consideration of joint custody legislation survives in the records of the debate in Illinois which occurred in 1982. In Illinois, joint custody was permitted by courts even in the absence of authorizing legislation, but the 1982 bill made that explicit. The debate, however, was interspersed with discussion of many other matters, especially a proposal to safeguard grandparents' rights to visitation, which attracted more attention than the joint custody proposal in both the Senate and House.[61] In 1985, a more comprehensive bill was adopted that allowed Illinois courts to order joint custody when they felt it in the best interests of the child, even if one of the parents objected (although in practice that was an unlikely result). During the senate debate no opposition was voiced, and after several of the sponsors had briefly spoken in favor of the bill, the impatience of other members was reflected by one senator: "Mr. President, is anybody against this? Well, what are we doing? We're going to be here forever, and . . . nobody . . . everybody . . . doesn't have to talk on everything."[62] Joint custody then passed by a vote of 59–0.

Conclusion

Thus the historical preference for maternal custody gave way in one state after another to joint custody arrangements. In most it occasioned little debate; the uncertainties of the novel arrangements never led a legislative body to sponsor research or to undertake a comprehensive examination of existing studies and the opinions of contemporary experts. By the mid-1980s, joint custody had become almost as "natural" and unquestioned an arrangement as paternal control had been 150 years earlier.

In no instance did the debate over joint custody spill beyond the limited set of intensely concerned proponents. Like the other changes in divorce law, joint custody required no public expenditures and did not impose an identifiable financial burden on the private sector. Experts played a much smaller role than in the case of no-fault or marital property reforms because widely recognized expertise was generally lacking even among mental health professionals. Once the empirical basis for Goldstein, Freud, and Solnit's support of maternal custody had crumbled, no consensus existed among child welfare specialists on the preferred handling of custody matters. The consequence in this instance was that the set of active participants was narrowed to the most active proponents of the change.

Whether by design or by accident, conflict over joint custody was successfully averted. It passed state legislatures as one of those bills that few cared enough to oppose because it promised substantial benefits and its potential harm was difficult to demonstrate.

9

The Consequences of Divorce Law Change

The political process creating reforms intricately molds their consequences. Mobilization of interests and resources often breeds groups and public institutions which shoulder the responsibility for administering or monitoring new policy. Moreover, the manner in which reformers define their mission endows a reform with a set of prescribed goals which later are used to help define success or failure. At the same time, the objectives articulated by the reformers also distinguish anticipated consequences from the unanticipated and unintended results which usually accompany change. Each of these effects may be observed with the changes in divorce law we have outlined.

The Absence of an Institutional Residue

The reform of divorce did not create new institutions. The new laws themselves did not establish new government agencies with responsibility for implementing the changes they incorporated. The political activity accompanying reform did not beget new interest groups with a special concern for monitoring the effects of the changes which they brought about.

In institutional terms, the divorce process was left much as it had been before the surge of reform began. Efforts to establish counseling bureaus and specialized family courts were rejected almost everywhere because of their expense and out of institutional jealousy by existing courts. Consequently, the implementation of divorce law remained principally in the hands of attorneys and their clients. It remained their responsibility to forge agreements consonant with the new laws and to bring the completed agreements to court for final approval. Judges took a leading role in implementing the new laws only in the small number of cases in which spouses could not reach a voluntary agreement. In all the others, judges simply approved what was placed before them with no more than a cursory glance at its contents. Thus, whether fault was really excluded in the negotiation of divorce agreements in no-fault states depended on how lawyers bargained on behalf of husbands and wives. The fault of one party could no longer be used in court, but it is likely that it occasionally colored the bargaining process as one party manipulated the guilt which often accompanies divorce. Likewise, while equitable distribution of marital property became the governing rule in most states and was defined by a long list of criteria, the spouse less eager for the divorce could threaten delay and thereby gain a larger settlement than might might ordinarily be awarded in court.[1]

The lack of institutional responsibility for the new laws led to an extreme decentralization of responsibility for implementation, with every law office and divorce counselor providing whatever interpretation they saw fit. Unlike laws which government agencies implement, divorce laws were left without bureaucratic supervision. With administration of the law left in the hands of a multitude of private attorneys, it is likely that considerable variation occurred in the manner in which the new laws were interpreted to clients.[2] These circumstances also resulted in a lack of external scrutiny of the laws' implementation because it occurred in private law offices where no outside observers watched. Unless one party later complained to a court or an agreement could not be reached in private negotiations, public officials were not involved in the enforcement of the new divorce laws.

In addition, no one had responsibility to collect information about the manner in which the new policies were working. Statistical information about divorces has always been in short supply in the United States. The courts grant divorces, but courts collect only minimal information on the cases they process.[3] Most states require their courts to send a brief statistical form to an office of vital statistics which is typically located in the state's department of health and which has very little interest in divorce. No other public agency had a stake in collecting systematic data which might indicate how the new laws were working. Thus, in states that permit both fault and no-fault divorce, no reports exist which would indicate what proportion of couples uses no-fault, although there are indications that its invocation is far from universal.[4] Neither did any state collect information about the division of property or the award of maintenance, making it difficult for anyone to determine whether the changes dictated by marital property provisions have been implemented. Finally, the changes in child custody law were not accompanied by a mandate to report custody awards, and no statistics exist to indicate how many joint and how many sole custody awards are made. Moreover, many couples alter their custody agreements informally when it seems convenient to the parents or the children, and unless one of the parents complains to a court, such changes remain unknown to public authorities. Consequently, no one knows the extent to which the new laws have changed custody arrangements for the divorcing population.

Another result of the lack of institutional concern about the new laws was the absence of publicity to potential users of the laws. Unlike campaigns to notify the public about new seat belt requirements, revised tax code revisions, or the altered availability of public assistance to pay utility bills, the novel divorce laws generated nothing but silence. A couple contemplating divorce depended almost entirely on their attorneys for information. Before meeting their attorneys, they were unlikely to encounter facts about new waiting periods under no-fault, about new property division rules under marital property codes, or about new child custody presumptions. Thus it was not uncommon for a husband to express surprise that "his" business was part of the couple's marital property subject to his wife's claim, and for a wife to be incredulous upon learning that her husband had a good chance to obtain joint custody if he wanted it.

Private groups did not fill the institutional void. The process by which these laws were adopted did not spawn private agencies to help citizens comply with them. The laws made no provision for governmental sponsorship of groups as the War on Poverty had done through the Community Action Program. Moreover, because there were no government agencies other than courts responsible for the law's enforcement, none took the initiative to form clientele groups which might help implement the laws; no parallel to the Farm Bureaus which had flourished under the patronage of the Department of Agriculture developed in the divorce field.

The absence of an institutional residue thus has had a profound effect on the implementation of divorce law reform. Neither public agency nor interest group took responsibility. No public body collected information about it. The new policies were left to flourish or wither with whatever attention the matrimonial bar devoted to them.

The Criteria of Success

The goals that reformers articulate define the measures that typically are first used to evaluate a new policy. This occurs because most reforms are suggested to repair performance gaps of old policies. For instance, poverty programs were urged by the Johnson administration in the 1960s to reduce the number of people living at the poverty level; they were then often evaluated in terms of that goal. The same was true of the new divorce laws. A key argument in favor of no-fault divorce was that it would eliminate fraud and decrease the bitterness of divorce actions; subsequently, it made sense to evaluate no-fault utilizing these objectives as benchmarks. The goal of joint custody was to increase fathers' participation in the lives of their children after divorce and to improve their record of paying child support; it was to be measured by the amount of paternal concern and the record of child support payments for fathers with joint custody. Thus the debate leading to adoption of reforms helped set the terms of its initial evaluation.

In the same manner, unintended results are defined by the adoption processes. Everything that falls outside the bounds of the planned results identified by supporters during the adoption campaign becomes unanticipated consequences. The fact that they are unanticipated reflects the characteristics of the people who became involved during the policy's adoption and their narrow concerns. For instance, the dominance of lawyers among no-fault advocates meant that anticipated consequences were procedurally oriented while the potential concerns of women would fall into the unanticipated category; and when it was later discovered that no-fault might have harmful financial consequences for women, such effects would be classified as unintended. Unanticipated consequences are usually pictured as costly mistakes because they are often revealed by later opponents of the policy. Unanticipated favorable consequences generally remain hidden because few people are motivated to discover or publicize them.

The choice of one criterion over others is also a function of group interests that were articulated during the adoption process. Groups active during the adoption campaign automatically are legitimized as evaluators of its success. They are the first to be asked by media representatives to comment and they are the most likely to review the reform after some experience with it. For instance, the divorce policies we have examined were largely the product of lawyers and were mostly implemented by them. Their control over the implementation process resulted in a tendency to evaluate the policies almost entirely from a legalistic perspective, at least in the first instance. In order for other groups to establish competing criteria—which often leads to the revelation of unanticipated or adverse results—they must edge themselves into the policy arena and stake a claim for attention. Moreover, groups which were not part of the adoption process are less likely to have gained positions in the implementation stage which would permit them to monitor the effects of the new policy.

This had particularly important implications for feminist groups. They had not been active in the consideration of no-fault, played no role in its implementation, and did not set the criteria for its evaluation. Thus, the first complaints about its impact on women were likely to come from feminist attorneys who, because of their dual role, were able to observe the law's consequences from a competing perspective and could claim some legitimacy in making their assessment. Their complaints, however, were relegated to the category of unanticipated consequences and they had to struggle to demonstrate the legitimacy of their concern, whereas the concern of the reformers about the law's impact on fraud and conflict diminution had automatic legitimacy.

Thus, our concern with the politics of adoption does not end with the acceptance of a policy. What we know (or indeed can reasonably learn) about the effects of policy changes is in large part influenced by the processes leading to their adoption. It is, therefore, useful to review that process for what it may tell us about the implementation process before examining our knowledge of those results themselves.

The Consequences of the Politics of Divorce Law Revision

We have repeatedly noted that the political process leading to divorce law revision occurred mostly in the shadow of more newsworthy events. More divisive problems consistently eclipsed divorce in the late 1960s and 1970s: the civil rights movement, race riots, Vietnam, Watergate, abortion, tax "revolts," and crime. Divorce law reform never became a partisan issue or a question in election campaigns; no high public official rose to prominence or fell into oblivion because of his stand on divorce policy. The principal implementational consequence of that obscurity was that the criteria for success or failure were narrowly defined by the reformers who produced the new policies. Few outsiders were invited to contribute alternative perspectives. The general public was never mobilized to concern itself with divorce law changes during election campaigns, when the general public is most likely to be attentive to policy issues. Those who had experienced divorce and those who might resort to it in the future did not help define the issues. The obscurity of divorce law revision thus minimized public attention toward implications of the changes, and many of them were perceived by legislators and the media as technical legal matters.

With little publicity and no mass support, the changes in family law also generated little media interest for following their consequences. Editors were unlikely to look back and ask, "What ever happened after . . . ?" Investigative journalists did not focus on the consequences of the new divorce laws.

Moreover, most of the attorneys active in the movement to change divorce laws were by professional training and organizational context fundamentally uninterésted in monitoring the changes they had wrought. The National Conference of Commissioners on Uniform State Laws (NCCUSL), for instance, had no machinery for continuing its concern with the Uniform Marriage and Divorce Act (UMDA) once it was formulated and published. The special committee which drafted the UMDA disbanded upon adoption of its product. No successor committee sought to collect evidence on the success or failure of its product. The individual attorneys and legislators active in changing marital property laws and custody standards were similarly disinclined to examine the consequences of their work. Individual attorneys active in the reforms turned to their private practices and collected only impressionistic evidence based on the cases they handled about the effects of the new laws. Legislators typically turned to other issues in the absence of complaints about divorce laws. Thus no mechanism existed for examining the effects of the changes.

Having indicated what was absent in the adoption process, we need, however, to be equally attentive to the evaluation consequences of some of the forces that produced the changes. Among the traits that had particularly important effects were the compatibility of the innovations with existing law, the activities of advocates of change, and the special character of interest-group efforts.

The compatibility of the innovations with existing law led to deflated expectations about the consequences of change. The new divorce laws rarely were trumpeted as ushering in a new era of family relationships. Their advocates' claims were more modest: no-fault would reduce conflict, marital property would recognize contemporary economic conditions, and joint custody would validate the father's post-divorce role. No-fault provisions reflected practices already incorporated by some divorcing couples in their negotiated agreements and accepted by legal practice. Martial property concepts seemed little more than a logical extension of existing case law and statutes which had slowly developed in many states. Even joint custody built on existing family structure. Thus, these threatened few and promised only moderate alterations. Advocates did not over-sell their reforms with great expectations which might later be dashed.

The characteristics of the advocates were central to the adoption of no-fault and joint custody legislation. Some were experts with little other involvement in the political arena; others were legislators who seized the opportunity to champion a policy which they found congenial and which already had considerable latent support. The legislators rarely contributed novel ideas to the proposals because others had already formulated the legislation through a national organization such as the NCCUSL (in the case of no-fault), a fathers' rights group (for joint custody laws), or some other state (in both instances for late adopters). Rather, their task was to maneuver the proposal through a state legislature. That required considerable political skills, such as prodding committee chairpersons, bringing supportive witnesses to hearings, avoiding potential opposition by minimizing publicity (yet not so much as to reduce the satisfaction of sponsorship), negotiating compromises over amendments, and obtaining a favorable review in the governor's office so that the governor would sign the bill into law. Most legislative proposals founder in this maze of procedures; the success of divorce law sponsors indicates that they possessed a high level of legislative skills.

Yet their work did not reflect an intense commitment to divorce reform which would lead to their continued involvement after the laws were passed; their job was to get a new law on the books, not to make sure that it worked in the way they intended. Nor did the sponsors of divorce law reform operate in the framework of established legislative coalitions. They built their own ad hoc groups of backers which dissolved once the bill had passed. These circumstances led them to move quickly to other issues once their divorce bill passed; in many cases, the divorce bill was not one of their major projects, because these entrepreneurs also worked on other bills, some of which required greater efforts and won them more acclaim.[5]

Finally, interest group participation was narrow rather than broad. Political analysts are accustomed to crediting interest groups with a large role; here they spoke only a few lines in the play. The most prominent supporters of many of these changes were lawyers, who usually worked through the family law section of their state bar association. Lawyers and the state bar were, however, peculiarly disinterested in implementation. They regarded the changes as permissive, enabling them to counsel clients to adopt new negotiation strategies and authorizing judges to consider new forms of remedies, such as joint as opposed to sole custody. They presumed that the courts would provide the required monitoring. If, over the course of several years, trial courts systematically misinterpreted the new statutes, the remedy would be an appellate decision or remedial legislation. Appellate litigation, however, was the responsibility of individual clients and attorneys. Remedial legislation would come about in response to concrete complaints to the family law section and to legislators; such complaints might reach them through analyses by law professors or law students in one of the law reviews published in the state. Thus lawyers and the state bar usually took a distinctly passive and reactive stance toward evaluating the reforms they had sponsored.

Sometimes an opposition group wins a significant role in implementing a policy as part of a compromise in the adoption process, as has been true of the medical profession's role in the medicare and medicaid programs. But that was not the case in divorce law reform. The principal opposition to no-fault was the Catholic church, and once it lost the fight it had little interest or leverage to influence its implementation. While the church continued to preach to its members against divorce on any grounds and discouraged its adherents from using divorce, its hold on Catholic lawyers was tenuous and insufficient to persuade them to alter their professional practices. After all, if a Catholic lawyer refused to recommend no-fault divorce to a client, the client might easily go to a non-Catholic attorney. In addition, since the administration of the new laws occurred in the privacy of law offices, neither the church nor any other opposition group had an opportunity to intervene in its implementation. When a case came to court, such groups lacked standing to intervene, because only persons immediately involved in the divorce could become a party to such a suit.

Other groups were similarly handicapped. Feminist organizations, as we have seen, generally lacked the will as well as the occasion to affect the implementation of new divorce laws. Individual feminists called attention to what they saw as adverse consequences, but they had no leverage to alter the laws' implementation. Men's rights groups were in a similar situation. Like some feminists, they responded to concerns provoked by individual cases, but they also did not systematically monitor the administration of the new laws and did not have a voice in their implementation.

Thus evaluators of the new laws could write on an almost empty slate. They were likely to begin with the objectives of the laws' proponents as a standard of success or failure. However, because even the laws' advocates withdrew from the combat after the laws were adopted, evaluators could bring with them their own preconceptions and biases with little fear of challenge. That is what occurred. Two kinds of evaluations resulted. One came from the legal community and principally examined intended outcomes through legal analyses; they represented the reaction of insiders to the new laws. The second primarily emanated from nonlegal academics and reflected the response of outsiders. We shall take a critical look at each.

Insider's Evaluations

No-Fault

Given the structure of the divorce process, lawyers were almost the only insiders who might evaluate the impact of the new divorce laws, and their opinions reflected the legal community's procedural concerns. They examined no-fault from the perspective of its effects on fraud and "unnecessary" conflict; they tested the laws by the criterion of legal precision, that is, whether the new laws imposed unambiguous standards; they concerned themselves primarily with expected results rather than unanticipated consequences.

Legal observers generally gave good marks to no-fault. Concentrating on the objectives that were widely shared in the legal community, later observers generally concluded that no-fault had achieved its goals of reducing fraud and stress. In Iowa an evaluation concluded:

The most significant accomplishment of the Act, as noted by the satisfied majority both of the judges and the attorneys, was the elimination
of the specific fault-based grounds for divorce; this resulted in a more
honest and civilized approach void of the fraud, perjury, and abuse
other parties frequently employed in divorce proceedings under the
old law. On balance, Iowa's "no-fault" dissolution of marriage statute has accomplished much of what its advocates had claimed for it.
With a few minor statutory adjustments and with a relatively minor
change in attitude by a few judges and lawyers, the Iowa dissolution
process can achieve its entire goal—to provide a just, expeditious, and
quiet termination of those marriages which society has no legitimate
interest in preserving.[6]

A Nebraska assessment is perhaps the clearest example of
how legislative deliberations molded the law's evaluation. The
authors examined each of the major arguments raised in favor
of or in opposition to the no-fault law when it was before the
legislature.[7] They addressed the goal of quelling unnecessary
animosity, and noted that two-thirds of the district judges in
Nebraska responding to a questionnaire agreed that no-fault
had lessened animosity between divorcing parties. They then
asked whether the new law led to an appropriate scrutiny of
divorce petitions by the courts, and questioned whether the
law had produced divorce by consent or unilateral demand.
The author's conclusions were that very little judicial scrutiny
occurs, that consenting parties could get their divorce as had
previously been true for uncontested fault divorces, and that
one party might unilaterally insist on a divorce under Nebraska's law. However, none of these conclusions troubled the
evaluators.[8]

Perhaps the greatest anxiety among lawyers about no-fault
divorce was that the standard of "irretrievable breakdown"
was too vague, a complaint already voiced by the American
Bar Association's Family Law Section when it considered the
Uniform Marriage and Divorce Act. There was also some concern that the hostility of adversarial, fault divorces would be
transferred to custody fights or disputes over property settlements.[9] Evaluations noted some misgivings about divorce
becoming "easy" to obtain, and that no-fault divorce undermined conventional views of marriage by doing "violence to
people of ordinary decent quality" because it eliminated fault

grounds,[10] a view that was shared by an assessment of California's no-fault law.[11]

Three characteristics of lawyers' evaluations of no-fault laws are particularly noteworthy. One is their paucity: legal scholars and practitioners simply took for granted that the new laws were working well and commissioned few assessments of their handiwork. The second is the limited scope of their appraisals. The handful of evaluations that were published simply took the objectives of the reformers as their guide and examined the degree to which their goals had been met. They were usually insensitive to unintended consequences. Third, the assessments which were published were based on limited data. Typically they encompassed only a single state and reflected impressions of purportedly informed observers and participants. No legal observer undertook large scale analysis of no-fault divorce in action.

Marital Property

Property law changed, as we saw, more gradually with less well articulated goals among its proponents than no-fault divorce. Marital property provisions were mostly an attempt to accommodate the social changes created by the massive entry of women into the labor market. The spread of marital property concepts and the demise of distribution according to title were intended to reflect the new social conditions in which many married women engaged in paid work outside the home and contributed not only housework but also monetary income to the family economy. Evaluations of the change emanating from legal scholars were much more critical of this change than they were of no-fault. The critiques were written almost entirely by women law professors who were sensitive to variations among women to a much larger extent than had been the legislatures and courts which devised the new rules. For instance, Mary Ann Glendon argued that the new rules were written basically for the exceptional rich rather than for the more numerous couples who had few assets to divide; they did little to compensate working-class wives at divorce. Moreover, she asserted that the large amount of discretion permitted to judges under the equitable division rule "throws divorcing spouses—and their children—into a lottery whose outcome greatly depends on the luck of the judicial draw and the competence of counsel, and in which the only sure winners are the lawyers."[12]

Glendon's assertions corresponded to more detailed examinations of New York's equitable distribution in the comment that ". . . the equitable distribution law has not been applied as intended,"[13] and Wisconsin's marital property provision about which Fineman concluded: "The reform has been successful on a symbolic level, but this success has been at the expense of more instrumental concerns."[14] These assessments were based largely on impressionistic evidence and on analysis of selected court cases. They drew on the analytic skills of lawyers rather than on economic and statistical analyses of large numbers of cases. Nevertheless, they had a broader scope than the evaluations of no-fault. They articulated the views of feminist activists (Fineman and Cohen) whose interests had purportedly been represented in the adoption of the reform, or the complaint of an outsider (Glendon) who sought to bring a new perspective into the ongoing debate on equal treatment of women. Notably absent from these evaluations were assessments of the impact of these changes on men, on new family formation through remarriage, or on children. Unlike the debates a century earlier when the Married Women Property Acts had been adopted, the marital property law changes in the twentieth century drew little comment on creditor-debtor relationships or their impact on families' ability to preserve their wealth.

Joint Custody

Joint custody laws were the newest addition to the law of divorce but quickly drew many commentators seeking to evaluate their impact. Unlike the glacial pace of property law change, joint custody emerged like a volcanic eruption and rapidly attracted widespread attention. As with the property laws, women attorneys were among the first to evaluate their impact by directing withering criticism at it. Suddenly, mothers' claims to their children were challenged in law if not in fact, and they responded vehemently. The critical commentators paid little attention to the purported objectives of joint custody to increase the involvement of fathers with their children and the supposed benefits of such a development. Rather, they presumed that fathers would continue to play only a small role in their children's lives and would seek joint custody primarily to wound their former wives and to reduce their child support obligations. Thus, one set of commentators argued that the effect of joint custody was to provide an opportunity for fathers to harass their ex-wives and to push them ever deeper into poverty by reducing their child support in proportion to the amount of time they spent with their children.[15] Such attacks on the new laws challenged the presumptions about gender equality that legislators had uncritically accepted as evidenced by the critique of a feminist lawyer who commented:

Inattention to the question of primary caretaking tends to devalue and in fact negate the traditional maternal role. . . . Sex neutrality should never be interpreted to mean that the traditional father role, even modified by small amounts of assistance to the mother, is as valuable to the child's development as the traditional mother role of primary nurturance, care, and responsibility.[16]

The feminists who criticized joint custody were usually lawyers with a foot in each camp; as lawyers they were insiders, while as feminists they were outsiders. They were attempting to reopen and expand the debate to new issues. They noted the potential financial consequences which had not attracted much attention during the legislative consideration of these laws. They cast doubt on the motives of fathers seeking joint custody and on their ability to provide the nurturance conventionally extended by mothers to their children. They questioned whether couples would be able to set aside their antagonism toward each other and create the cooperative environment required by joint custody arrangements.

The evaluations produced by feminist lawyers were based on the same kinds of information that guided lawmakers. They relied upon impressions and anecdotes, sometimes buttressed by examination of selected court cases. Like the proponents of divorce law change, the evaluators did not undertake broad empirical analyses of the actualities facing divorcing couples as they encountered the new laws.

Evaluations by Outsiders

Only a few outsiders noticed the changes in divorce laws and bothered to examine them. This was despite the fact that a substantial body of empirical data was being accumulated and examined by economists indicating the adverse effects of divorce upon women.[17] Those studies showed that the economic position of women deteriorated drastically after divorce in terms of their income and their assets. The effects were most adverse for older women who had been married for many years and who suddenly had to rely upon their own wage-earning capacity; they were also severe for mothers of young children. However, the authors of these analyses did not concern themselves with the potentially beneficial or adverse consequences of the new laws which were being implemented as the studies were underway.

The most prominent social scientist to examine those potential effects was a feminist sociologist, Lenore Weitzman. Beginning in the middle 1970s, she and her associates published a series of articles which analyzed both the impact of divorce and the effects of recent legal changes. Their analyses usually appeared in law reviews rather than social science journals, but they reported empirical research. Their work culminated in a book called *The Divorce Revolution,* which attracted wide attention in the public media and among policy makers as well as in the scholarly community.[18]

Weitzman examined California's experiences with no-fault, which had been adopted in 1969; with equal division of property, which had also been adopted in 1969 as California already was a community property state; and with joint custody, which had been adopted in 1979. Weitzman interviewed divorced men and women in Los Angeles, she reviewed approximately 2500 court records from both Los Angeles and San Francisco, and she spoke to many California matrimonial lawyers and judges.[19] In addition, she relied on studies undertaken by other scholars.

Weitzman had a decidedly jaded view of the consequences of the new laws, even though she found that "the no-fault reforms have generally had a positive effect on the divorce process: there is clearly less hostility and acrimony and, on the whole, all of our respondents—California men and women, and lawyers and judges—express positive feelings about the no-fault law."[20] However, she concluded that no-fault divorce had altered the marriage relationship in a fundamental way by legitimizing temporary unions instead of emphasizing the life-long character of marriage.[21] Thus, the legal tradition no longer supported the expectation that marriage was for life, but rather encouraged the view that marriages were a temporary convenience which could easily be shed. In addition, the new laws, according to Weitzman, tilted the scales against women. Wives lost an important bargaining chip when they could no longer obstruct their husbands' divorce plans under no-fault; moreover, they lost their status as the innocent party claimed by many under fault procedures. As she put it:

Even though many divorced women were not very well off after divorce under the old law, the levers of fault and consent gave them some power to bargain for a better financial settlement. The reformers did not realize that without these levers women would need alternative provisions in the law to enable them to negotiate adequate financial settlements.[22]

She reported that wives often received less money under the new laws than under the old because they sometimes had obtained more than half the community property as the innocent party under the old laws. Weitzman claimed that under the new laws they usually got less than half. Moreover, in about one-third of the cases, they lost the family home because it was sold to divide the proceeds.[23] Yet, with half the equity from their former home, most wives could not purchase another comparable home and were instead forced into the high-rental market that characterized California in the 1970s.[24]

The change in alimony and child custody laws also worked to the disadvantage of many ex-wives, according to Weitzman. Maintenance, as it was now called, rarely lasted for more than a few years and did not suffice for older women who could not establish themselves in the job market.[25] Changing custody laws permitted a father to challenge his wife's claim to their children more readily and gave him a bargaining chip to negotiate a property settlement or a child support schedule more favorable to him.[26]

In sum, according to Weitzman the new laws, although intended to place husbands and wives on an equal footing, left women holding an empty grocery bag. They usually retained physical custody of their children but received reduced financial assistance. As a result, the per capita income of the wife's fragment of the family (she and her children) decreased dramatically after the divorce, while the ex-husband enjoyed a dramatic gain in his per capita income because he often lived alone immediately after the divorce and did not have to share his earnings. This led to a 42% increase in the standard of living for divorced men approximately one year after divorce, while divorced women suffered a 73% decline.[27] Weitzman concludes that the changes which occurred in divorce law in California and the rest of the country constituted an unmitigated disaster for women.

Another study by Elizabeth Peters, an economist, buttressed Weitzman's conclusions.[28] Peters used a very large national sample that had been constructed for the Census Bureau. She found that in states where "unilateral" divorces were available, divorcing women received less alimony, child support, and property than in states where such divorces were unavailable. She attributed the differences to the effects of the new no-fault divorce laws.

Closer examination of both Weitzman's and Peters's results, however, leaves doubts about the strength of their conclusions. Weitzman's conclusions may be challenged because they were based primarily on California's peculiar experiences. As we have seen in the preceding chapters, the legal changes that occurred in California were not blindly copied elsewhere. California was one of only fourteen states with a pure no-fault law; everywhere else, fault divorces remained available. California was one of only five states with equal distribution of property, and it was one of only eight which began the reform period with community property rules. In most other states, the pool of property available for distribution expanded from the property to which wife alone held title to an equitable distribution of everything accumulated during the marriage. In addition, some states specifically protected the custodial parent's claim to the family home, a provision which California did not adopt. Finally, the joint custody rules adopted across the nation showed considerable variation.

Thus it is incorrect to presume, as Weitzman and some of her readers did, that the experiences of California women would necessarily be replicated in other portions of the nation. The changes adopted elsewhere may have improved the legal claims of women much more than they did in California.[29]

In addition, there is no clear empirical support for Weitzman's assertion that the new laws have undermined old views of marriage. It is true that divorce rates rose sharply during the period that no-fault divorce and the other divorce law changes were being made. However, every study of the impact of these laws on divorce rates has concluded that no relationship existed between the introduction of no-fault and the rise in divorce.[30] This appears to be true even for California, where the number of divorces jumped from 81,500 just before no-fault to 112,900 the year after.[31] The explanation rests in the fact that divorce rates were increasing even in the absence of no-fault procedures, and many of the "extra" divorces just after the introduction of no-fault in California can be attributed to the more rapid processing of divorces under the new law. Thus, no-fault itself did not add to the rising wave of divorce.

Weitzman's conclusions regarding the effects of joint custody also seem to be premature. Only the most preliminary research results are available for an evaluation of joint custody. One study based on Colorado data indicates that joint custody fathers have a better record of paying child support than fathers without joint custody, but the authors themselves indicate that several confounding factors, such as the job stability of these joint custody fathers and the fact that they volunteered for such an arrangement, might be the true cause for their better payment record.[32] There are no analyses of changes in fathering under those arrangements. However, a handful of studies have examined some other issues. The largest existing study, conducted in Canada, indicates that there is a very high degree of parental satisfaction with joint custody arrangements, especially among those who voluntarily entered into such agreements rather than being forced into them by the divorce court.[33] This and another study of California custody cases indicate that few joint custody cases return to court to iron out subsequent difficulties; the relitigation rate seems to be lower than when sole custody is awarded.[34] These studies, however, have been unable to trace the fate of joint custody arrangements for a long period of time as children mature, or as parents remarry or move to another location. Moreover, none of them ask children their judgment of these arrangements or compare clinical evaluations of children living under sole or joint custody arrangements. The Canadian study suggests that fathers there have not used joint custody to escape financial responsibilities that might otherwise be imposed on them; the American studies have not yet addressed that question.

Other kinds of problems surround Peters's findings. While they are not based on the experience of a single state, her classification of states by their legal rules combines states who *only* have no-fault with many that have *both* fault and no-fault divorce laws. Thus the effect of no-fault is somewhat blurred. Moreover, the effects she finds are quite small. According to her analysis, unilateral divorce reduced alimony by $186 per year, child support by $462 per year, and property settlements by $137; each of these effects was statistically significant at the .10 confidence level. Thus, while Peters's analysis provides support for Weitzman's findings, that support is weak; one might also conclude that the effect of the new laws as reflected in the census data is quite small.

There is good reason to expect an inconsequential result. As we have seen, there was no systematic connection between no-fault and alimony, child support, and property settlement rules. For no-fault to produce an adverse or beneficial effect upon women, most lawyers and judges would need to interpret these rules in a systematically biased fashion, and the independent effect of the new rules about property division, alimony, child support, and child custody would have to be overwhelmed by such interpretations. So far no one has examined the independent consequences of these other legal changes. Rather, all divorce reform has been bundled into the fault/no-fault dichotomy, which our previous chapters show to be a gross oversimplification.

Despite such reservations, Weitzman's results were immediately acclaimed by a wide range of observers and had the effect of expanding the political arena of divorce law reform. Weitzman's conclusions alarmed many feminists and mobilized them to examine the impact of divorce laws on women. As one feminist reviewer put it, "One person's freedom is another's disaster."[35] In California, Weitzman's book led to the establishment of a legislative study group and the introduction of a large number of bills to remedy the defects she had perceived.[36] It is unlikely that, after her work, divorce law reformers can present their proposals as technical solutions to procedural problems. The problems facing women and children have been so clearly highlighted that all future revisions of divorce law face the challenge of showing that the effects of new alterations will not be adverse.

Conclusion

Divorce law reform, despite feminist critiques, will probably be counted a success. Those who promoted the reforms have largely succeeded in dictating the terms of their evaluation. By those standards, most of the changes have had their intended effects: less fraud and hostility in the divorce process, greater equality in the division of assets, and more opportunities for fathers to remain involved with their children. The unanticipated consequences are perhaps not so much adverse effects as incomplete achievements, magnified by the habituation of Americans to divorce which has multiplied its adverse effects on women and children. The changes we have chronicled were not intended to perfect the lives of divorced women and their children. While recent reforms perhaps have not worsened their situation, they also have not sufficiently improved it.

The new awareness that divorce law is not just a technical domain of lawyers but deals with social problems of deprivation and impoverishment creates an entirely different political climate for new reforms. It is unlikely that lawyers will dominate the next set of reforms as they did the last. Nor is it probable that feminists and advocates for children will remain outsiders in considering new changes. It is quite possible that the next proposals will not be considered through the routine policy process; instead they are likely to attract widespread attention and generate considerable conflict.

10

Routine Policy Making and Divorce

This book has had two themes: divorce law reform and the characteristics of the routine policy-making process. The course of divorce law reform during the last two decades cannot be understood without an appreciation of the routine policy-making process. Although routine policy processes operate in many more arenas than those we have described here, the characteristics of divorce reform help illuminate its distinctive traits.

Neither routine policy making in general nor the divorce law revisions in particular involved trivial alterations of public policy. Despite the claims of its advocates to the contrary, the new divorce laws fundamentally altered the face of divorce proceedings in the United States. While divorces were easy to obtain before the new laws came into force, as the rising divorce rates of the 1960s suggest, and were made still more accessible by these laws, other elements of the divorce process were affected more significantly.

Before no-fault, even uncontested divorces centered around imputations of fault and guilt, and those allegations often made a difference with respect to the division of property and custody of children. That has changed. Fault has been banished from most proceedings, and new criteria have been established to justify who gets what after the divorce.

Those new provisions emphasize to a much larger degree than ever before the contribution of women to the economic welfare of the family. It is an exaggeration to call the new laws egalitarian because most of them urge an equitable rather than an equal distribution of assets. In most courts that is likely to mean that the husband's labor will continue to be valued more highly than the wife's, especially if he has developed "his own" business while she labored at home. With a considerable lack of realism, the new laws often presume that women are fully able to earn their own living, even though the labor market continues to pay women less than men and makes it difficult for women to enjoy the same career successes as men. Nevertheless, the new laws conclude that ex-husbands have only a transitory responsibility for their former wives' welfare after divorce. However, the new laws have planted the seeds for more equal treatment of women by explicitly recognizing the economic value of their homemaking and childrearing efforts. It may take many years for economic opportunities to match the gender neutrality of family law, but those legal provisions provide a necessary legitimation of women's roles outside the home. Moreover, by freeing women from the responsibility of being the family's exclusive childrearer and recognizing the legitimacy of joint responsibilities through acceptance of joint custody, the law has taken an important step in restructuring post-divorce family arrangements. All of these changes aim at core values in American family life. Thus, we cannot say that divorce law reform merely rearranged existing practices or provided trivial additions to an existing body of law.

However, the objectives of the new laws' advocates were usually much more modest. They had a limited vision of their reforms and did not seek to change the world. In most cases, they saw their proposals as technical alterations of existing procedures. While they were embarrassed by the fraud seemingly inherent in divorce proceedings, the legal profession and courts had lived with it for a very long time and there was no urgency to their reform. Indeed, against the background of the truly pressing social and political crises of the 1960s and 1970s, divorce reform appeared as a very humble project.

Moreover, the proponents of divorce law reform usually sought to portray their schemes as a mere updating to match existing practice. It was important to them to claim that the bills they were advocating were compatible with the law already on the books or with the law in action. That assertion reduced the perceived risk in adopting the new laws. Although little empirical evidence could be adduced to predict their likely effects, their compatibility with existing practice reduced the apparent uncertainty that normally attaches to innovative procedures.

The success of the reformers was phenomenal, particularly in view of the fact that they were not an organized group seeking a common goal. Despite their failure to organize a national movement, they succeeded in obtaining similar legal provisions across the entire nation. As we have seen, some form of no-fault became available within every state; most states adopted some form of marital property; and almost half the states accepted joint custody. All of this happened in less than two decades. Few highly organized reform movements can claim such success in American history, yet these alterations were not the product of an organized movement.

Divorce reformers succeeded because they adopted tactics which accommodated the routine policy-making process. I have no evidence that this was a conscious maneuver; rather, it seems that the advocates of divorce law reform intuitively took advantage of opportunities which they recognized but which they had not fully conceptualized. Eight tactical elements constituted their strategy.

First, the proponents of reform narrowly defined both the problem they addressed and the solutions they proposed. Instead of claiming that they sought to solve a crisis of massive proportions, they talked of matters which concerned the bench and bar but did not seem to impinge substantially on the general population. This was most marked in their advocacy of no-fault divorce and the definition of marital property. Advocates of divorce law reform deliberately eschewed exaggeration of their efforts. They did not seek to save the world; they only sought to improve the administration of justice.

Consequently, they succeeded in achieving the second element of a routine policy-making strategy by limiting interest group participation. In part that was luck, because the feminists who might otherwise have been attracted to divorce law reform were preoccupied with the Equal Rights Amendment, abortion, and other issues, and the Catholic church was distracted with its internal liberalization after Vatican II. However, the avoidance of broader interest-group participation was also the consequence of the restrictive definition of the problem and of calculated efforts to avoid trouble with other interests, as the actions of the California reformers demonstrated. During the 1960s and 1970s, an era which celebrated "community participation," divorce law reformers managed to keep their project under the control of a very limited set of activists.

Third, this set of activists often claimed a special prerogative to mold the new divorce laws because of their expertise with the legal system. Divorce laws, especially those dealing with property, were obscure and complex and seemed to need the expertise that only lawyers could supply. Even mental health professionals played only a minor role in devising the new laws, even when the proposed rules dealt with the fate of children rather than property. Consequently, the new divorce laws were largely the product of the legal profession.

Fourth, the new laws as adopted seemed to cost no one anything. Some of the original proposals had been somewhat more ambitious in aspiring to establish counseling services or new family courts. The cost of those suggestions, however, led to their rejection or early demise. What remained were new policies which appeared free of any cost. They imposed no new public expenditures because they simply rearranged existing procedures which required no new personnel. They also did not appear to inflict costs on private parties because they promised to simplify proceedings rather than complicate them. Although assets might be distributed in somewhat different ways, these effects were not highlighted and did not alarm any potential interest.

Fifth, the advocates of the laws usually claimed that their project either involved simply the codification of law that already existed in scattered statutes or in appellate decisions, or it consisted of bringing the state's law into conformity with practice elsewhere. In both instances, the proponents could claim that their bills would be compatible with existing law rather than constituting radical innovations. They mostly emphasized continuity rather than originality.

The stress on compatibility with existing law produced the sixth element of their strategy, which was to reduce the perceived risk and uncertainty attaching to their recommendations. Proposed divorce law reforms were presented as low-risk ventures because they involved only marginal changes in existing practices either in one's own state or in others. Those who sought a pure no-fault law could point to Iowa as well as California as places where it worked without appearing to produce special problems. Most of the states, however, preferred a more cautious approach which was even less uncertain and risky; they simply attached no-fault to their list of fault grounds for divorce. When advocates of marital property drafted their bills, they often borrowed language from other states or from appellate decisions to reduce the uncertainty that new verbiage might encourage. Finally, the advocates of joint custody did not insist on making it the only, or even the preferred arrangement; in most states they were satisfied with establishing the legitimacy of such custodial agreements.

The emphasis on compatibility with existing law and the low risk of the new endowed the proposals with a high degree of legitimacy, the seventh element of the advocates' strategy. Incremental change that did not threaten uncertain results enjoyed the legitimacy of existing law. Several characteristics of the reforms added to the persuasiveness of this claim. One was the imprimatur of legal experts; another was an appeal to fundamental social values, such as the assertion that joint custody did nothing more than reinforce fathering among ex-husbands. Finally, these reforms were scrupulously adopted within accepted legislative procedures. No attempt was made to slip them into the legal code through some administrative maneuver or procedural legerdemain.

The eighth characteristic of the routine policy strategy of divorce reformers was to keep a low public profile. No attempt was made to increase the media appeal of the reformers' efforts. They worked in the deep shadow of obscurity and flourished there. Thus the fourth estate, which plays such a prominent role in conflictual policy making, was almost excluded from the process. With few exceptions, neither newspapers nor electronic media granted more than an occasional mention to divorce reform efforts or outcomes. Such a strategy was easier to pursue in the state capitols where divorce laws were adopted than in Washington, because the media pay much less attention to the activities of state legislatures than to

Congress. The success of reformers in avoiding publicity reinforced their effort to maintain control in the hands of experts and to limit the number of interest-group participants.

The routine policy-making process thus fits the divorce reform effort extraordinarily well. However, it would be mistaken to think that it was invented by the divorce reformers. The routine policy process is perhaps the dominant process at both the state and national level. In Congress, the procedure used to pass such measures is the consent calendar, on which are found not only private bills but also proposals which no member of Congress wishes to block. Writing about such noncontroversial bills, one observer notes: "Many, many legislative measures fall into this sort of category."[1] In the states, the routine policy-making process has been described (without its being given this name) in the adoption of child abuse legislation[2] and in the passage of criminal law reforms.[3] For instance, Heinz and his collaborators concluded that "the politics of criminal law in Illinois has been characterized by . . . conflict minimization,"[4] while Berk, Brackman, and Lesser wrote of California that "the social structure shapes the interests, beliefs, and resources of all citizens who, in their routine actions and in a variety of spheres, produce consequences for the criminal justice system."[5] It has been described in another guise by scholars examining the policy-making routines of municipal bureaucrats who make decisions about which streets to pave, how often garbage will be collected, and where parks will be located.[6] In those instances, the policy-making arena is the bureaucracy rather than the legislature, and consequently bureaucrats play a central role in the process.

The routine policy process, while dominated by well-located, intensely motivated participants, is necessarily less populist than conflictual policy-making processes. Players in the routine process succeed in monopolizing influence only as long as they avoid stirring up competing interests and attracting public attention. Although on the surface the process may appear undemocratic, it appears instead to provide a means for accommodating narrowly defined but intensely advocated interests, and for adopting noncontroversial policies even when conflictual policy processes are stalemated. The routine policy process may, therefore, be a safety valve which permits policy making to proceed despite the many obstacles erected by the fragmentation of the American federal system, the separation of powers, the paralysis of parties, and the hyperactivity of interest groups which is so often observed in American politics.

There is a price for this result. It may have surprised many readers that feminists were not responsible for the transformation of American divorce law. Many simply assume that divorce is a woman's issue and that, since the change in divorce laws coincided with the rise to prominence of feminist organizations, the new divorce laws would be the product of their agitation. As we have repeatedly shown, however, feminists stood on the sidelines during most of the activities that led to the adoption of these laws, and the interests of women in general were poorly represented during their consideration. We have indicated many reasons for the failure of feminists to articulate their concerns, among them the pace of feminism's own development, its focus on other issues, and the ambivalence displayed by some feminists toward the issues involved in divorce law reform. In addition, however, we may point to the routine policy process, which sought to exclude interests groups like feminists. Movement groups thrive on controversy and visibility so that their members may be mobilized; routine policy making follows the opposite strategy of avoiding confrontation and publicity.

Finally, the content of the new divorce laws combined with the high divorce rate of the 1980s carry within them the seeds of a quite unexpected intervention of government in the lives of American families. Family life is generally considered to be private; American homes are private castles. That remains true for those families whose lives have not been disrupted by divorce. Divorced men and women and their children, however, operate under an entirely different set of rules. How they handle their property becomes subject to the law of marital property distribution. For an increasing number, divorce agreements even govern how they dispose of their homes. Intact families exercise almost sovereign power in deciding their life-styles, but that is not true for the divorced, one of whom must pay an amount set by their agreement or by the court to the other spouse for maintenance or child support; obversely, those receiving such payments have their life-styles fixed to a considerable degree by the way in which divorce law is applied to them. Even the right to move to another location is affected by divorce law for divorced parents. Whether they have joint or sole custody, they often must obtain permission from a court to move to a distant location,[7] and in some cases they receive permission only at the price of losing custody. Children of divorce also live under different rules. They may move out of one parent's household and into another's, an option not available to children of intact marriages. On the other hand, the level of support is not simply a matter of private bargaining within the confines of the family but may involve recourse to the power of strangers in the courtroom. In many instances, the failure of divorce agreements to foresee college costs may mean that the children of divorce are deprived of the college education they would otherwise have obtained.[8]

None of these results were contemplated by the architects of the new divorce laws. Yet, with the prevalence of divorce among American families, these special rules will breach the privacy of an increasing number of American homes.

Appendix

The following indicates the individuals I interviewed and the archives I used. I am enormously indebted to them for their assistance. However, their listing here or their mention in the notes to the text does not imply an endorsement of the interpretation I have given to the events they described.

List of Interviews

Marshall Auerbach, 19 August 1984
Edmund G. Brown, 3 June 1985
Gordon Burrows, 2 May 1985
Karen Burstein, 30 March 1985
James Cook, 5 June 1987
David Crystal, 12 February 1985
Richard Dinkelspiel, 12 February 1985
Harry Fain, 3 June 1985
Henry H. Foster, 4 January 1985
Robert Frederick, 3 October 1985
Doris Jonas Freed, 4 January 1985
Kathryn Gehrels, 16 July 1984
Aiden Gough, 12 February 1985
Allan J. Greiman, 10 July 1984
Donald Grunsky, 13 February 1985
James Hayes, 4 June 1985
Bernard Hellring, 2 May 1985
Herma Hill Kay, 11 February 1985
Jimmy M. Lago, 1 August 1984
Robert J. Levy, 8–9 November 1984
William Marovitz, 26 October 1984
John McCabe, 26 October 1984

Robert Mnookin, 17 July 1984
May Newburger, 3 May 1985
Jeffrey O'Connell, 10 September 1985
Julia Perles, 4 January 1985
Richard D. Schwartz, 8 June 1984
Phillip Shaefer, 5 January 1985
Elizabeth Shaw, 12 October 1985
Loren Sloan, 12 October 1985
Percy E. Sutton, 3 March 1985
Stuart Walzer, 3 June 1985
Jerome Wilson, 3 January 1985

Archives Used

Des Moines Register, Des loines, Iowa, clippings file.

Iowa State Archives, Des Moines, Iowa. Materials regarding Divorce Laws Study Committee.

Levy Papers. Personal papers relating to work of the National Conference of Commissioners on Uniform State Laws in the possession of Robert J. Levy.

National Conference of Commissioners on Uniform State Laws, Chicago, Illinois. Transcripts of debates.

Schlesinger Library, Radcliffe College, Cambridge, Massachusetts. Papers of the National Organization for Women relating to divorce, File P10.

University of California, Berkeley. Government History Documentation Project, oral histories of Edmund G. Brown, Sr. and Ronald Reagan administrations.

Notes

Chapter One

1. U.S. Bureau of the Census, *American Families and Living Arrangements,* Current Population Reports, Special Studies, Series P–23, No. 104 (Washington, May 1980). Chapter 2 discusses these changes in greater detail.

2. Caleb Foote, Robert J. Levy, and Frank E. A. Sander, *Cases and Materials on Family Law* (Boston: Little, Brown & Co., 1966), 297–302

3. Nancy E. McGlen and Karen O'Connor, *Women's Rights: The Struggle for Equality in the Nineteenth and Twentieth Centuries* (New York: Praeger, 1983), 293–94.

4. Chapman v. Mitchell, 23 N.J. Misc 358 at 359–60, 44 A.2d 392 at 393; cited in John D. Johnston, Jr., "Sex and Property: The Common Law Tradition, the Law School Curriculum, and Developments Toward Equality," *New York University Law Review* 47 (1972): 1089.

5. Norma Basch, *In the Eyes of the Law: Women, Marriage, and Property in Nineteenth-Century New York* (Ithaca, N.Y.: Cornell University Press, 1982) describes in detail the status of women in the early nineteenth century and the passage of these laws in New York. Also see Chapter 7 below.

6. Lynne Carol Halem, *Divorce Reform* (New York: Free Press, 1980), 16–48 describes the state of divorce law in the nineteenth century. See also, Elaine Tyler May, *Great Expectations: Marriage and Divorce in Post-Victorian America* (Chicago: University of Chicago Press, 1980).

7. Lawrence M. Friedman, *A History of American Law,* 2d ed. (New York: Simon and Schuster, 1985), 498–506.

8. Max Rheinstein, *Marriage Stability, Divorce, and the Law* (Chicago: University of Chicago Press, 1972), 10–22.

9. B. H. Lee, *Divorce Law Reform in England* (London: Peter Owen, 1974), 3–24; Friedman, *History,* 204.

10. Shapiro v. Thompson, 394 U.S. 618 (1969).

11. Analyses of governmental intervention in family life may be found in Elizabeth Pleck, *Domestic Tyranny: The Making of Social Policy against Family Violence from Colonial Times to the Present* (New York: Oxford University Press, 1987), and Michael Grossberg, *Governing the Hearth: Law and the Family in Nineteenth-century America* (Chapel Hill: University of North Carolina Press, 1985).

12. Linda Gordon, "Child Abuse, Gender, and the Myth of Family Independence: Thoughts on the History of Family Violence and Its Social Control 1880–1920," *New York University Review of Law & Social Change* 12 (1983–1984): 523–37.

13. Viviana A. Zelizer, *Pricing the Priceless Child: The Changing Social Value of Children* (New York: Basic Books, 1985), 169–207.

14. On both, see Friedman, *History,* 561.

15. For example, Illinois Revised Statutes, Chapter 40, par. 513: "The Court may make such provision for the education and maintenance of the child . . . , whether of minor or majority age, out of the property or income of each or both parents;" Utah: Harris v. Harris, 585 P2d 435 (1978); Wyoming: Broyles v. Broyles, 711 P2d 1119 (1985). Moreover, in many states, agreed decrees which provide for child support to pay for college fees are enforceable.

16. Anne L. Spitzer, "Moving and Storage of Postdivorce Children: Relocation, The Constitution, and the Courts," *Arizona State Law Journal* 1985 (1985): 1–78; Katherine C. Sheehan, "Post-Divorce Child Custody and Family Relocation," *Harvard Women's Law Journal* 9 (1986): 135–52.

17. Alan Rosenthal, "Soaking, Poking, and Just Wallowing in It," *PS* 19 (1986): 848.

18. Malcolm M. Feeley and Austin D. Sarat, *The Policy Dilemma: Federal Crime Policy and the Law Enforcement Assistance Administration 1968–1978* (Minneapolis: University of Minnesota Press, 1980); Virginia Gray and Bruce Williams, *The Organizational Politics of Criminal Justice* (Lexington, Mass: Lexington Books, 1980).

19. David A. Rochefort, *American Social Welfare Policy: Dynamics of Formulation and Change* (Boulder, Colo.: Westview Press, 1986).

20. John W. Kingdon, *Agendas, Alternatives, and Public Policies* (Boston: Little, Brown & Co., 1984).

21. For example, see Barbara J. Nelson, *Making an Issue of Child*

Abuse: Political Agenda Setting for Social Problems (Chicago: University of Chicago Press, 1984).

22. Kingdon, *Agendas.*

23. David J. Garrow, *Protest at Selma: Martin Luther King, Jr., and the Voting Rights Act of 1965* (New Haven: Yale University Press, 1978).

24. Jane J. Mansbridge, *Why We Lost the ERA* (Chicago: University of Chicago Press, 1986).

25. Raymond A. Bauer, Ithiel de Sola Pool, and Lewis Anthony Dexter, *American Business and Public Policy: The Politics of Foreign Trade* (New York: Atherton Press, 1963).

26. The role of Howard Jarvis in generating tax limitations in California and other states is typical. See Susan B. Hansen, "The Politics of State Taxation," in Virginia Gray, Herbert Jacob, and Kenneth N. Vines, eds., *Politics in the American States,* 4th ed. (Boston: Little, Brown & Co., 1983), 440–53. For another example, see Michael J. BeVier, *Politics Backstage: Inside the California Legislature* (Philadelphia: Temple University Press, 1979).

27. Typical of this genre is Thomas R. Dye, *Politics, Economics and the Public* (Chicago: Rand McNally, 1966).

28. James G. March and Johan P. Olsen, *Ambiguity and Choice in Organizations* (Bergen, Norway: Harald Lyche, 1976).

29. Alan Rosenthal and Rod Forth, "The Assembly Line: Law Production in the American States," *Legislative Studies Quarterly* 3 (1978): 265–91.

30. Ibid., 274.

31. This estimate is based on a count of pages in each state's Session Laws (or equivalently titled volume) and an estimate of the number of words based on a random sample of pages.

32. Laws of New Mexico, 1979, Chapter 279.

33. Laws of New Mexico, 1979, Chapter 82.

34. Georgia Laws, 1979 Session, No. 611.

35. Laws of Florida, Chapter 75–262.

36. Laws of Florida, Chapter 75–130.

37. Some analysts, such as Barbara Nelson, would focus on the inherent characteristics of issues and therefore, for instance, look for issues which are valence-like because they are associated with "a single, unified set of civic values" (Nelson, *Child Abuse,* 28) and others which are position-like. (Ibid., 26–29.) I have not opted for this approach because I believe that issue characteristics are pliable and are the object of manipulation by those who advance or oppose particular proposals. I find it more fruitful to think of consensual or conflictual processes rather than consensual or conflictual issues.

38. Robert Cobb, Jennie-Keith Ross, and Marc Howard Ross, "Agenda Building as a Comparative Political Process," *American Political Science Review* 70 (1976): 126–38.

39. Paul Burstein, *Discrimination, Jobs, and Politics* (Chicago: University of Chicago Press, 1985).

40. Cobb, Ross, and Ross, "Agenda Building."

41. Nelson, *Child Abuse,* 14.

Chapter Two

1. U.S. Bureau of the Census, *Historical Statistics of the United States, Colonial Times to 1957* (Washington, 1960), 25; U.S. Bureau of the Census, *Statistical Abstract of the United States, 1982–83* (Washington, 1982), 71.

2. U.S. Bureau of the Census, *Historical Statistics,* 24; U.S. Bureau of the Census, *Statistical Abstract 1982–83,* 64.

3. U.S. Bureau of the Census, *Statistical Abstract 1982–83,* 65.

4. Ibid., 41.

5. U.S. Bureau of the Census, "Marital Status and Living Arrangements: March 1981," Current Population Reports, Series P-20, No. 372 (Washington, June 1982), 5.

6. Claudia Goldin, "The Earnings Gap in Historical Perspective," in *Comparable Worth: Issue for the 80's: A Consultation of the U.S. Commission on Civil Rights* (Washington: GPO, 1984), 5.

7. Howard Hayge, "Rise in Mothers' Labor Force Activity Includes Those with Infants," *Monthly Labor Review* 109 (February 1986): 44.

8. Ibid.

9. Suzanne M. Bianchi and Daphne Spain, *American Women in Transition* (New York: Russell Sage Foundation, 1986), 160.

10. Ibid., 231.

11. Glenna Spitze and Scott J. South, "Women's Employment, Time Expenditure, and Divorce," *Journal of Family Issues* 6 (1985): 307–29; Andrew Cherlin, "Employment, Income, and Family Life: The Case of Marital Dissolution," *Women's Changing Roles at Home and on the Job: Proceedings of a Conference on the National Longitudinal Surveys of Mature Women,* U.S. Department of Labor Special Report No. 26 (Washington, September 1978), 157–78; Elizabeth M. Havens, "Women, Work, and Wedlock: Female Marital Patterns in the United States," *American Journal of Sociology* 78 (1973): 975–81.

12. Bianchi and Spain, *American Women in Transition,* 202.

13. Ibid., 227.

14. Viviana A. Zelizer, *Pricing the Priceless Child: The Changing*

Social Value of Children (New York: Basic Books, 1985), 64–112.

15. Ibid., 169–207.

16. Joseph H. Pleck, "Men's Power with Women, Other Men, and Society," in Elizabeth H. Pleck and Joseph H. Pleck, eds., *The American Man* (Englewood Cliffs, N.J.: Prentice-Hall, 1980), 429; Daniel Yankelovich, "The Meaning of Work," in Jerome Rosow, ed., *The Worker and the Job* (Englewood Cliffs, N.J.: Prentice-Hall, 1974).

17. Quoted in John Demos, *Past, Present, and Personal: The Family in the Life Course of American History* (New York: Oxford University Press, 1986), 32.

18. Georgia Duerst-Lahti, "Building an Infrastructure for the Woman's Movement: Intergovernmental Structures and Dynamics 1963 to 1969," typescript in author's files, 1987.

19. Jo Freeman, *The Politics of Women's Liberation* (New York: David McKay, 1975), 54–56.

20. Paul Burstein, *Discrimination, Jobs, and Politics: The Struggle for Equal Employment Opportunity in the United States since the New Deal* (Chicago: University of Chicago Press, 1985), 22–23.

21. One of those instances is recounted by Jeanne C. Marsh, Alison Geist, and Nathan Caplan, *Rape and the Limits of Law Reform* (Boston: Auburn House, 1982).

22. William Eich, "Gender Bias in the Courtroom: Some Participants Are More Equal Than Others," *Judicature* 69 (April–May 1986): 339–43; Lynn Hecht Schafran, "Documenting Gender Bias in the Courts: The Task Force Approach," *Judicature* 70 (February–March 1987): 280–90.

23. The role of NOW and the feminist movement in family law reform is analyzed by me in "Women and Divorce Reform," in Patricia Gurin and Louise Tilley, eds., *Women in Twentieth Century American Politics* (New York: Russell Sage Foundation, 1988 [forthcoming]).

24. The focus on children and companionship roughly parallels two of the categories delineated by Ernest Mowere, *The Family, Its Organization and Disorganization* (Chicago: University of Chicago Press, 1932), 98.

25. George Gallup, Jr., *The Gallup Poll: Public Opinion 1985* (Wilmington, Del.: Scholarly Resources, 1986), 111.

26. Jessie Bernard, *The Future of Marriage*, 2d ed. (New Haven, Conn.: Yale University Press, 1982), 126 quotes a 1945 family textbook, Burgess and Locke, as follows:

The companionship concept of marriage (with its emphasis upon affection, comradeship, democracy, and happiness of members of the family) is replacing the old-time notion of marriage as a relation stressing respect, obedience, authority and duty. This new concept has arisen as the result of many factors, including the loss of economic and other functions by the family, the growth of the urban way of life, the rising status of women, the continued decline in parental control of children's marriage, and the application of democracy in marital and familial relations.

E. W. Burgess and Harvey J. Locke, *The Family* (New York: American Book Co., 1945).

27. Lynne Carol Halem, *Divorce Reform: Changing Legal and Social Perspectives* (New York: Free Press, 1980).

28. Andrew J. Cherlin, *Marriage, Divorce, Remarriage* (Cambridge: Harvard University Press, 1981).

29. Paul C. Glick, "Marriage, Divorce and Living Arrangements," *Journal of Family Issues* 5 (March 1984): 7–26; Samuel H. Preston, "Estimating the Proportion of American Marriages That End in Divorce," *Sociological Methods and Research* 3 (May 1975): 435–60.

30. These trends and international comparisons are summarized in Joni Seager and Ann Olson, *Women in the World: An International Atlas* (New York: Simon and Schuster, 1986).

31. The Gallup data come from George H. Gallup, *The Gallup Poll* (New York: Random House, 1971); the 1974 data are from the General Social Survey, and were retrieved for me by Thomas W. Pavkov.

Chapter Three

1. Norma Basch, *In the Eyes of the Law: Women, Marriage, and Property in Nineteenth-Century New York* (Ithaca, N.Y.: Cornell University Press, 1982) discusses these developments in detail.

2. Brigitte M. Bodenheimer, "The Utah Marriage Counseling Experiment: An Account of Changes in Divorce Law and Procedure," *Utah Law Review* 7 (1961): 443–77; Louis H. Burke, "The Role of Conciliaton in Divorce Cases," *Journal of Family Law* 1 (1961): 209–27; Julius M. Kovachy, "The Evolution of Ohio Divorce Laws: Their Development to Meet Present Day Needs," *Western Reserve Law Review* 5 (1953): 62–77.

3. Lynne Carol Halem, *Divorce Reform* (New York: The Free Press, 1980), 22–23.

4. Ibid., 25–26.

5. Ibid., 35.

6. Ibid., 40; Lawrence M. Friedman and Robert V. Percival, "Who Sues for Divorce? From Fault Through Fiction to Freedom," *Journal of Legal Studies* 5 (January 1976): 40.

7. Halem, *Divorce Reform*, 129–34, 222–26.

8. Friedman and Percival, "Who Sues," 65.

9. State of New York, *Report of the Joint Legislative Committee on Matrimonial and Family Laws*, Legislative Document no. 8, 31 March 1966, 21.

10. Hubert J. O'Gorman, *Lawyers and Matrimonial Cases* (New York: The Free Press of Glencoe, 1963), 29.

11. Most of the plaintiffs—by arrangement—were women, since rich women could spend an idle six weeks more readily than their husbands.

12. Nelson M. Blake, *The Road to Reno: A History of Divorce in the United States* (New York: Macmillan Co., 1962).

13. O'Gorman, *Lawyers and Matrimonial Cases*, 12.

14. One author claimed that there were 150 grounds for annulment in New York (Blake, *Road to Reno*, 197, citing Joseph R. Clevenger).

15. Ibid., 15, 189–202.

16. Ibid., 203–25.

17. Interview with an attorney who wished to remain anonymous.

18. Baker v. Carr, 369 U.S. 186 (1962).

19. For a discussion of Spellman's political influence, see John Cooney, *The American Pope* (New York: Times Books, 1984).

20. Phillip H. Schaefer, interview with author, New York, N.Y., 12 May 1985.

21. Jerome Wilson, interview with author, New York, N.Y., 3 January 1985.

22. Henry H. Foster, interview with author, New York, N.Y., 4 January 1985.

23. Robert S. Bird, "Divorce—New York Style," *New York Herald Tribune*, 14–19, 21 November 1965.

24. Several professional associations of lawyers existed in New York at the time. The Bar Association of the City of New York was the most exclusive group, consisting almost entirely of men who had large commercial practices.

25. Interviews with Phillip H. Schaefer (see note 20) and Henry H. Foster (see note 22).

26. State of New York, *Report of the Joint Legislative Committee on Matrimonial and Family Laws*, 1 December 1965, typescript, 643–44.

27. State of New York, *1966 Report on Matrimonial and Family Laws*, 54ff. The Chief Judge of New York's highest court also supported compulsory conciliation. Hearings, 670.

28. Laws of New York, 1966, Chapter 254.

29. Percy Sutton, interview with author, New York, N.Y., 30 March 1985.

Chapter Four

1. Terry Christensen and Larry N. Gerston, *The California Connection* (Boston: Little, Brown & Co., 1984), 127–34.

2. Kristin Luker, *Abortion and the Politics of Motherhood* (Berkeley: University of California Press, 1984).

3. Lynne Carol Halem, *Divorce Reform: Changing Legal and Social Perspectives* (New York: Free Press, 1980), 84–157.

4. California Assembly Interim Committee on the Judiciary, Transcript of Proceedings on Domestic Relations, 8–9 October 1964, Los Angeles, typescript, 31.

5. *Putting Asunder: A Divorce Law for Contemporary Society,* A Report of a Group Appointed by the Archbishop of Canterbury in January, 1964 (London: S.P.C.K., 1966), 39.

6. Ibid., 41.

7. Herma Hill Kay, "An Appraisal of California's No-Fault Divorce Law," *California Law Review* 75 (January 1987): 298.

8. Lawrence M. Friedman and Jack Ladinsky, "Social Change and the Law of Industrial Accidents," *Columbia Law Review* 67 (January 1967): 50–82.

9. Interview with a participant who wished to remain anonymous and with Jeffrey O'Connell (by telephone), one of the authors of the no-fault automobile insurance plan, 10 September 1985.

10. Herma Hill Kay, interview with author, Berkeley, Ca., 11 February 1985.

11. Other grounds available in California in 1969 were willful neglect, habitual intemperance, conviction of a felony, and insanity. California Civil Code §92 (1872) and California Statutes 2547, Chapter 951, §2 (1941). Both are cited in Herma Hill Kay, "Equality and Difference," *Cincinnati Law Review* 56 (1987): 28, notes 115, 119.

12. DeBurgh v. DeBurgh, 39 C2d 858 (1952) at 872. The case did not establish no-fault but discussed the criteria of "a total and irremedial breakdown of the marriage" in the context of limiting the recrimination defense. That doctrine had allowed a defendant to offer proof that the plaintiff was as much at fault as he and therefore neither should get a divorce.

13. Gerald Zaltman, Robert Duncan, and Jonny Holbek, *Innovations and Organizations* (New York: John Wiley & Sons, 1973), 5.

14. Ibid., 55–58.

15. James G. March and Johan P. Olsen, *Ambiguity and Choice in Organizations* (Bergen, Norway: Harald Lyche, 1976), 26–27.

16. Referring to equality between men and women, Herma Hill Kay wrote: ". . . that theme was not part of the earlier studies and deliberations that had produced the [Family Law] Act." Kay, "Equality and Difference," 44.

17. The California legislature met every two years; when it was not in session, interim study committees worked to examine the need for new legislation. The interim judiciary committee was such a study group.

18. Kay attributes the resurgence of interest in the California legislature to a bachelor legislator, who as a lawyer was disturbed by lack of uniformity in divorce decisions. Kay, "Equality and Difference," 4.

19. California Assembly Interim Committee on the Judiciary, Transcript of Proceedings on Domestic Relations, 8–9 January 1964, Los Angeles, typescript, 182.

20. California Assembly Interim Committee on the Judiciary, Transcript of Proceedings on Domestic Relations, 8–9 October 1964, Los Angeles, typescript, 38.

21. Ibid.

22. Ibid., 39.

23. Kay interview, 11 February 1985.

24. Governor's Commission on the Family, Final Report, 15 December 1966, typescript.

25. Kay, "Equality and Difference," 37–38, note 175.

26. Governor's Commission Final Report, 5.

27. Ibid., 7.

28. Ibid., 23.

29. Ibid., 26, 32.

30. Ibid., 46.

31. Ibid., 112.

32. Ibid., 38–43.

33. Ibid., 29.

34. This account is based largely on my interviews with Herma Hill Kay on 11 February and with Aidan Gough, Santa Clara, Ca., on 12 February 1985.

35. Kay, "Equality and Difference," 39.

36. Ibid.

37. Donald Grunsky, interview with author in Watsonville, Ca., 12 February 1985.

38. The changes are extensively discussed by Kay, "Equality and Difference," 41–44.

39. For instance, I found a petition in Grunsky's files from the San Rose Diocesan Council of Catholic Women recommending "that the basic provisions of the Family Law Act be incorporated into the bill to

be voted by the legislature and that this constructive legislation which promotes the stability of the family, the basic unit of society, be passed."

40. It has also been widely noted that Hayes himself was going through a divorce and may have molded some elements of the new law to help his case. Kay, "Equality and Difference," 44, note 213; Riane Tennenhaus Eisler, *Dissolution: No-Fault Divorce, Marriage, and the Future of Women* (New York: McGraw-Hill, 1977), 24–31.

41. See Sec. 4506(1) of Ch. 1608s, 1969 Regular Session.

42. Compare Sec. 051 of the Commission's Draft, p. 111 with Title 6, Sec. 4800 of Ch. 1608.

43. See Title 6, Sec. 4801.

44. Kay, "Equality and Difference," 43.

45. Title 4, Sec. 4600(a).

46. Title 8, Sec. 5101.

47. Title 8, Sec. 5105.

48. California's Advisory Commission on the Status of Women apparently supported no-fault divorce because it eliminated hypocrisy in the divorce process. Kay, "No-Fault Divorce," 300.

49. Cf. Kristin Luker, *Abortion and the Politics of Motherhood.*

Chapter Five

1. Paul Brodeur, *Outrageous Misconduct: The Asbestos Industry on Trial* (New York: Pantheon Books, 1985), 27–29.

2. A listing may be found in the annual publication of the National Conference of Commissioners on Uniform State Laws, *Handbook of the National Conference of Commissioners on Uniform State Laws and Proceedings of the Annual Conference Meeting* (Chicago: NCCUSL).

3. Robert E. Keeton and Jeffrey O'Connell, *Basic Protection for the Traffic Victim: A Blueprint for Reforming Automobile Insurance* (Boston: Little, Brown & Co., 1965).

4. Jeffrey O'Connell, telephone interview with author, 10 September 1985.

5. Herma Hill Kay, interview with author, Berkeley, Ca., 11 February 1985, and interviews with participants who wished to remain anonymous.

6. Among these were "Trends in Marriage and Divorce Laws in Western Countries," Law & Contemporary Problems 18 (1953): 3–19; "The Law of Divorce and the Problem of Marriage Stability," *Vanderbilt Law Review* 9 (1956): 633–64; "The Code and the Family," *The Code Napoleon and the Common Law World,* New York

Institute of Comparative Law (New York: New York University, 1956), 139–61; and "Divorce and the Law in Germany," *American Journal of Sociology* 65 (1960): 489–98. Rheinstein was also an influential teacher; among his students was Herma Hill Kay.

7. This portion of the intellectual roots of no-fault divorce is explored in detail by Lynne Carol Halem, *Divorce Reform: Changing Legal and Social Perspectives* (New York: Free Press, 1980).

8. The idea also began to appear in law school casebooks; see, in particular, Caleb Foote, Robert J. Levy, and Frank E. A. Sander, *Cases and Materials on Family Law* (Boston: Little, Brown & Co., 1966), 783–85.

9. The *Index to Legal Periodicals* for 1961–64 lists only three articles that appear to discuss no-fault divorce among the 150 articles listed under the heading "divorce." By contrast, a decade later, 41 of 161 such articles were about no-fault.

10. NCCUSL, *Handbook*, 1966 edition, 184–87.

11. These were summarized at the time by Robert J. Levy, "Uniform Marriage and Divorce Legislation: A Preliminary Analysis Prepared for the Special Committee on Divorce of the National Conference of Commissioners on Uniform State Laws," typescript, 1968, 42–49; henceforth referred to as Levy monograph.

12. Interviews with Robert J. Levy, 8–9 November 1984.

13. The grants are reflected in the treasurer's report of the conference as printed in the annual publications of the NCCUSL *Handbook* between 1968 and 1972.

14. Interview with a participant who wished to remain anonymous.

15. Levy Papers: Letter to Allison Dunham July 10, 1967.

16. Levy Papers: Letter from Robert J. Levy to Maurice Merrill, 15 November 1967.

17. Levy monograph, 167.

18. Levy papers: Letter from Alice Rossi to Robert J. Levy, 8 January 1969; Alice Rossi, letter to author, 18 September 1987.

19. Henry H. Foster, Jr., "Divorce Reform and the Uniform Act," *South Dakota Law Review* 18 (1973): 578, note 39. Additionally, Foster wrote: ". . . the Committee and its Reporters had little if any actual experience in matrimonial litigation."

20. Levy later wrote: "Each policy—indeed, each clause of each section—was the subject of intense, often cantankerous debate (among Commissioners on the Committee, between Advisors and Commissioners, and often between Commissioners and Reporters); indeed, I cannot recall any provision which was not the product either of a compromise among competing policy choices or a vote to which there was

significant dissent." Robert J. Levy, "Introduction," *South Dakota Law Review* 18 (1973): 533.

21. The debates are preserved in transcript form in the offices of the National Conference of Commissioners on Uniform State Laws, Chicago, Illinois.

22. This had not been true at the beginning of the process, when Levy raised a large number of broader social issues in his monograph.

23. Interview with a participant who wished to remain anonymous.

24. Robert J. Levy, "Comments on the Legislative History of the Uniform Marriage and Divorce Act," *Family Law Quarterly* 7 (1973): 409, note 10.

25. Harvey L. Zuckman, "The ABA Family Law Section v. the NCCUSL: Alienation, Separation and Forced Reconciliation over the Uniform Marriage and Divorce Act," *Catholic University Law Review* 24 (Fall 1974): 74.

26. Clarence Kolwyck, "The Ten-Year Struggle for a Section of Family Law," *Family Law Quarterly* 3 (1969): 269.

27. Foster, "Divorce Reform," 577–80.

28. Ibid., 575.

29. Ibid., 578.

30. Ibid.; American Bar Association, Family Law Section, "Report," typescript, 21 December 1970.

31. One may discern the changes by comparing the 1970 and 1973 drafts of the Uniform Marriage and Divorce Act as published in Editors of the Family Law Reporter, *Desk Guide to the Uniform Marriage and Divorce Act* (Washington: Bureau of National Affairs, 1974).

32. The debate is to be found in typewritten transcripts at the offices of the National Conference of Commissioners on Uniform State Laws, Chicago, Illinois.

Chapter Six

1. Doris Jonas Freed, "Grounds for Divorce in the American Jurisdictions as of June 1, 1974," *Family Law Quarterly* 8 (1974): 401.

2. The fifteen with the dates of adoption of no-fault were California (1969), Iowa (1970), Colorado (1971), Florida (1971), Michigan (1971), Oregon (1971), Kentucky (1972), Nebraska (1972), Arizona (1973), Missouri (1973), Washington (1973), Minnesota (1974), Delaware (1974), Montana (1975), and Wisconsin (1977).

3. Arkansas Acts 1937, No. 167; *Arkansas Statutes,* annotated

edition (Charlottesville: Michie Co., 1985), Title 34–1202. See also Parish v. Parish 114 S.W. 2d 29 (1938).

4. *Oklahoma Statues Annotated* (St. Paul, MN: West Publishing Co., 1961), with 1985 supplement, Title 12, Par. 1271.

5. *Vernon's Texas Codes Annotated* (St. Paul, Minn: West Publishing Co., 1975) with 1986 supplement, Title 3.01–08. See also McGinley v. McGinley 295 S.W. 2d 913 (1957).

6. Freed, "Grounds for Divorce," 422.

7. Ibid., 416, 419.

8. Ibid. A less assertive suggestion that states which provided divorce on the ground of separation were no-fault states had already been articulated in 1969; Doris Jonas Freed and Henry H. Foster, Jr., "Divorce American Style," *Annals of the American Academy of Political and Social Science* 383 (May 1969): 71–88.

9. Gerald Zaltman, Robert Duncan, and Jonny Holbek, *Innovations and Organizations* (New York: John Wiley & Sons, 1973), 7–8.

10. Ibid., 34; Jack L. Walker, "The Diffusion of Innovations Among the American States," *American Political Science Review* 63 (1969): 880–99; Virginia Gray, "Innovation in the States: A Diffusion Study," *American Political Science Review* 67 (1973): 1174–85; Richard Hofferbert, "Ecological Development and Policy Change in the American States," *Midwest Journal of Political Science* 10 (1966): 485.

11. Walker, "Diffusion of Innovations."

12. Joseph Gusfield, *Symbolic Crusade: Status Politics and the American Temperance Movement,* 2d ed. (Urbana: University of Illinois Press, 1986).

13. For a review listing of much of the literature on the civil rights movement, see John D. McCarthy and Mayer N. Zald, "Resource Mobilization and Social Movements: A Partial Theory," *American Journal of Sociology* 82 (1977): 1212–41.

14. For the California origins of the tax revolt movement, see Terry Christensen and Larry N. Gerston, *The California Connection* (Boston: Little, Brown & Co., 1984), 208–30; David O. Sears and Jack Citrin, *Tax revolt: Something for Nothing in California* (Cambridge: Harvard University Press, 1982).

15. George H. Gallup, *The Gallup Poll: Public Opinion, 1935–1971* (New York, Random House, 1972).

16. Ibid., 493.

17. Ibid., 1990.

18. Ibid.

19. General Social Surveys, 1972–1982, Chicago: National Opinion Research Center, July 1982. Question 172 and 173, p. 162.

20. For a description of this ferment of organizational activity, see Jo Freeman, *The Politics of Women's Liberation* (New York: David McKay Co., 1985).

21. Paul Burstein, *Discrimination, Jobs, and Politics* (Chicago: University of Chicago Press, 1985), 20–23 describes the circumstances under which this ban was adopted.

22. The absence of women and feminists during consideration of no-fault legislation is examined in greater detail in Herbert Jacob, "Women and Divorce Reform," in Patricia Gurin and Louise Tilley, eds., *Women in Twentieth Century American Politics* (New York: Russell Sage Foundation, 1988 [forthcoming]).

23. David B. Truman, *The Governmental Process* (New York: Alfred A. Knopf, 1951); Jeffrey M. Berry, *The Interest Group Society* (Boston: Little, Brown & Co., 1984).

24. Testimony of Peter Hoffman, chair, Legislative Committee, United States Divorce Reform, Inc., California Assembly Interim Committee on Judiciary, Transcript of Proceedings on Domestic Relations, 8–9 January 1965, 207.

25. James cook, interview with author in Los Angeles, 5 June 1987.

26. In some, however, no bar association activity was visible. That seems to have been true, for instance, in Oregon. See Roger J. Leo, "Oregon's No-Fault Marriage Dissolution Act," *Oregon Law Review* 51 (1972): 715–17.

27. "1973 Annual Report of Family Law Committee of the State Bar of Arizona," *Arizona Bar Journal* (Spring 1973): 58–59.

28. "Proposal for Revision of the Connecticut Statutes Relative to Divorce: Statute and Commentary," *Connecticut Bar Journal* 44 (1970): 411.

29. "Marriage, Divorce Law-Change Proposals OK'd by Board," *Washington State Bar News* 27 (February 1973): 13.

30. George E. Snyder, "Divorce Michigan Style—1972 and Beyond," *Michigan Bar Journal* (December 1981): 740.

31. "Section on Domestic Relations and Family Affairs," *Maine Bar Bulletin* 7 (1973): 8.

32. A Florida lawyer reassuringly ended his article on that state's no-fault law as follows: "One thing seems certain. The role of the family law practitioner is still a vital and important one, and he will still be needed." Keith E. Collyer, "The Marriage is Irretrievably Broken," *Florida Bar Journal* 45 (November 1971): 561. See also Harvey L. Zuckman, "The ABA Family Law Section v. the NCCUSL: Aliena-

tion, Separation and Forced Reconciliation over the Uniform Marriage and Divorce Act," *Catholic University Law Review* 24 (Fall 1974): 63, note 10.

33. Author interviews with Herma Hill Kay, Berkeley, Ca., 11 February 1985, and John McCabe, Chicago, Il., 26 October 1984, and interviews with participants who wished to remain anonymous. Kay, however, went to Wisconsin and conferred with feminist advocates of divorce reform, and McCabe lobbied in Illinois and South Dakota. "[I] would happily have done more if bills introducing the Uniform Act had been introduced. However, bills introducing the Uniform Act were few and far between, and still are, for that matter. That is the reason nobody did a lot of testifying." Letter from John M. McCabe to author, 14 August 1987.

34. Virginia Gray, "Innovation in the States"; also Jack L. Walker, "Innovation in State Politics," in Herbert Jacob and Kenneth N. Vines, eds., *Politics in the American States*, 2d ed., (Boston: Little, Brown & Co., 1971), 368–70.

35. See note 9 in Chapter 5 above.

36. Henry H. Foster, Jr., "Current Trends in Divorce Law," *Family Law Quarterly* 1 (1967): 21–40.

37. Caleb Foote, Robert J. Levy, and Frank E. A. Sander, *Cases and Materials on Family Law* (Boston: Little, Brown & Co., 1966), 783–85.

38. Susan Welch and Kay Thompson, "The Impact of Federal Incentives on State Policy Innovation," *American Journal of Political Science* 24 (1980) 715–29.

39. Henry Robert Glick, "Policy-Making and State Supreme Courts: The Judiciary as an Interest Group," *Law and Society Review* 5 (November 1970); 271–92.

40. John W. Kingdon, *Agendas, Alternatives, and Public Policies* (Boston: Little, Brown & Co., 1984), 129–30, 188–93.

41. Kristin Luker, *Abortion and the Politics of Motherhood* (Berkeley: University of California Press, 1984).

42. Donald Grunsky, interview with author, Watsonville, Ca., 13 February 1985.

43. I searched the records of these archives at the University of California, Berkeley.

44. Iowa State Archives.

45. See the following description of this legislation. It did not permit no-fault divorce but eliminated fault from property distribution and alimony decisions.

46. Author interviews in Chicago with Marshall Auerbach, 14 August 1984; Allen Greiman, 10 July 1984; Jimmy H. Lago, 1 August

1984; John McCabe, 26 October 1984; and interview with participant who wished to remain anonymous.

47. Richard M. Cyert and James G. March, *A Behavioral Theory of the Firm* (Englewood Cliffs, N.J.: Prentice-Hall, 1963), 278–79.

48. Walker, "Diffusion of Innovations."

49. Ibid.

50. Joseph Veroff, Elizabeth Douvan, and Richard A. Kulka, *The Inner American: A Self-Portrait from 1957 to 1976* (New York: Basic Books, 1981), 176.

51. The following account is based on records of the Divorce Study Committee in the Iowa State Archives and interviews with several of its members.

52. Divorce Laws Study Committee materials, Iowa State Archive, Des Moines, Iowa.

53. Based on author examination of the *Des Moines Tribune* and *Register* for 19 November 1969.

54. *Des Moines Register,* 11 February and 5 March 1970. The *Register* has a large circulation throughout the state of Iowa.

55. This account is based on author interviews with major participants in Chicago, including Marshall Auerbach, 14 August 1984; Allan J. Greiman, 10 July 1984; and Jimmy H. Lago, 1 August 1984; as well as contemporary reports in the *Chicago Tribune.*

56. Transcript of Debate on HB 697 on 23 June 1977.

57. Martha L. Fineman, "Implementing Equality: Ideology, Contradiction, and Social Change," *Wisconsin Law Review* 1983 (1983): 800.

58. Freed, "Grounds for Divorce," 420.

59. The following is based largely on Fineman, "Implementing Equality," 846–72.

60. Herma Hill Kay, interview with author in Berkeley, Ca., 11 February 1985.

61. Fineman cites the memorandum from McCabe, then legislative director of the NCCUSL. Fineman, "Implementing Equality," 870–71.

62. Jane J. Mansbridge, *Why We Lost the ERA* (Chicago: University of Chicago Press, 1986).

Chapter Seven

1. Note that according to Article 1, Section 2 of the U.S. Constitution, slaves counted only as three-fifths of a free person in the allocation of representation.

2. For instance, Adam Kuper, "African Marriage in an Impinging

World: The Case of Southern Africa," in Kingsley Davis, ed., *Contemporary Marriage: Comparative Perspectives on a Changing Institution* (New York: Russell Sage Foundation, 1985), 254–55; Margery Wolf, "Marriage, Family and the State in Contemporary China," in Davis, *Contemporary Marriage,* 223–26.

3. Carl Degler, *At Odds: Women and the Family in America from the Revolution to the Present* (New York: Oxford University Press, 1980), 140–42; Viviana A. Zelizer, *Pricing the Priceless Child: The Changing Social Value of Children* (New York: Basic Books, 1985), 56–72.

4. Norma Basch, *In the Eyes of the Law: Women, Marriage, and Property in Nineteenth-Century New York* (Ithaca, N.Y.: Cornell University Press, 1982), 27.

5. Peggy A. Rabkin, *Fathers to Daughters: The Legal Foundations of Female Emancipation* (Westport, Conn: Greenwood Press, 1980).

6. Basch, *In the Eyes of the Law,* 113–35.

7. Rabkin, *Fathers to Daughters,* 75.

8. Ibid., 91–117.

9. §3, Chap 200, 1848 Act as reprinted in Rabkin, *Fathers to Daughters,* 184.

10. Ibid.

11. Rabkin, *Fathers to Daughters,* 125–37.

12. Reprinted in Ibid., 187.

13. Ibid., 144–45.

14. Richard H. Chused, "Married Women's Property Law: 1800–1850," *Georgetown Law Review* 71 (1983): 1359–1425.

15. Basch, *In the Eyes of the Law,* 138; Rabkin, *Fathers to Daughters,* 91–98, indicates that at the New York State Constitutional Convention of 1846, the debate was more spirited and the vote close; two years later, the proposals breezed through the legislature.

16. Rabkin, *Fathers to Daughters,* 126–37, shows that most of the litigation spurred by these statutes involved husbands *and* wives against creditors rather than husbands versus wives.

17. Lawrence M. Friedman, *A History of American Law,* 2d ed. (New York: Simon and Schuster, 1985), 211.

18. See K. Melder, "The Beginnings of the Women's Rights Movement in the United States 1800–1840" (Ph.D. dissertation, Yale University, 1964); K. Thurman, "The Married Women's Property Acts" (LL.M. thesis, University of Wisconsin, 1966); John D. Johnston, Jr., "Sex and Property: The Common Law Tradition, the Law School Curriculum, and Developments Toward Equality," *New York University Law Review* 47 (1972): 1033–92; Rabkin, *Fathers to Daughters;* Elizabeth A. Cheadle, "The Development of Sharing Prin-

ciples in Common Law Marital Property States," *UCLA Law Review* 28 (1981); 1269–1313; and Basch, *In the Eyes of the Law*. The exception was Mary R. Beard, *Woman as Force in History* (New York: Macmillan & Co., 1946).

19. Rabkin, *Fathers to Daughters,* 106–17, and 156, asserts that the first of these laws was not primarily the product of feminist agitation; in fact, the 1848 law in New York and the preceding one in Mississippi were adopted before the Seneca Falls Women's Rights Convention of 1848. Rather, she argues that these laws spurred feminists to further activity in support of women's suffrage.

20. 18 Mich Stat. Ann. §25.103 (Supp. 1966), as quoted in Robert J. Levy, "Uniform Marriage and Divorce Legislation: A Preliminary Analysis Prepared for the Special Committee on Divorce of the National Conference of Commissioners on Uniform State Laws," typescript, 1968, Appendix B-8; henceforth referred to as Levy monograph.

21. They are Arizona, California, Idaho, Louisiana, Nevada, New Mexico, Texas, and Washington. Herma Hill Kay, "Equality and Difference: A Perspective on No-Fault Divorce and Its Aftermath," *University of Cincinnati Law Review* 56 (1987): 8, note 23.

22. Homer H. Clark, *Law of Domestic Relations* (Minneapolis, Minn.: West Publishing Co., 1968), 420–81.

23. Report of the Governor's Commission on the Family (1966), typescript, 44.

24. Clark, *Law of Domestic Relations,* 415–16.

25. Ibid., 450–51, as quoted in Levy monograph, 168–69.

26. U.S. Bureau of the Census, *Child Support and Alimony: 1978,* Current Population Reports, Special Studies Series P–23, no. 112 (Washington, September 1981).

27. Friedman, *History,* 209.

28. Gen. Stat. Kan. §4756 (1889), as cited in Cheadle, "Sharing Principles," 1295, note 141.

29. Cheadle, "Sharing Principles," 1297–99.

30. A search of both statutory and case law citations referring to the Kansas statutes showed that they were cited only in New Hampshire (Leonard v. Leonard 129 A. 725 [1925], Wyoming (Mann v. Mann 15 P.2d 478 [1932], and Alaska (Rhodes v. Rhodes 370 P.2d 902 [1962], and then only as authority for judicial discretion in dividing assets.

31. Cheadle, "Sharing Principles," 1299–1308.

32. Ibid., 1313.

33. Carl N. Degler, *At Odds,* 430.

34. Ibid., p. 434.

35. Levy monograph, 135.

36. Clark, *Law of Domestic Relations*.

37. Levy monograph, 164–86.

38. Report of the Committee on Civil and Political Rights of the President's Commission on the Status of Women (Washington: Government Printing Office, 1963), 18.

39. Levy monograph, 169–70.

40. Ibid., 167.

41. This seems to have been true for the following twelve states: Alabama, Delaware, Florida, Illinois, Kentucky, Michigan, Nebraska, New Hampshire, North Carolina, North Dakota, Ohio, and West Virginia. See Levy monograph, Appendix B.

42. Quoted by Levy monograph, Appendix B2–B3 for Alaska Stat. Ann., tit. 9, Ch. 55, art. 3, §09.55 210(6) (Supp. 1967).

43. Herma Hill Kay notes of 22 July 1968 meeting of committee in Philadelphia, Levy Papers.

44. Letter from Clarence Kolwyck to Robert J. Levy dated 10 April 1969 and 1970 letter from Dan Hopson to Robert J. Levy. Levy papers.

45. Levy Papers, Letter to Robert J. Levy, 8 January 1969.

46. Remarks by Bernard Hellring during 1973 debate over §307 of the 1973 draft of the Uniform Marriage and Divorce Act. Typewritten transcript of the debate available at the offices of the National Conference of Commissioners on Uniform State Laws, Chicago, Illinois.

47. Report of the Section of Family Law, American Bar Association, 21 December 1970, typescript, 15.

48. Uniform Marriage and Divorce Act, 1970 Act, as amended 1971 and 1973, §307.

49. Compare the 1970 and 1973 versions of the UMDA as published in the National Conference of Commissioners on Uniform State Laws, *Handbook* (Chicago: NCCUSL, 1970 and 1973).

50. Kay, "Equality and Difference," *Cincinnati Law Review* 56 (1987): 49.

51. On the origin of this provision, see Kay, "Equality and Difference," 42–43.

52. Uniform Marriage and Divorce Act, as amended 1973, §307, Alternative B.

53. Howard A. Krom, "California's Divorce Law Reform: An Historical Analysis," *Pacific Law Journal* 1 (1970): 156–81.

54. This evaluation is based on a reading of the relevant statutes for each of the fifty states. They are most conveniently found in various parts of each state's Annotated Code.

55. The states, with the year in parentheses, were: Arkansas (1979), Connecticut (1979), Colorado (1973), Delaware (1974), Illinois (1977), Indiana (1973), Iowa (1980), Kentucky (1972), Massachusetts (1977), Maryland (1978), Maine (1971), Missouri (1977), Nebraska (1972), North Carolina (1981), New Jersey (1971), New Mexico (1973), New York (1980), Oregon (1971), Pennsylvania (1980), Rhode Island (1979), Virginia (1982), Wisconsin (1977), and Wyoming (1977).

56. They were: Arizona, California, Colorado, Delaware, Idaho, Illinois, Indiana, Kentucky, Michigan, Minnesota, Mississippi, Montana, Nebraska, Ohio, Pennsylvania, South Dakota, Tennessee, Washington, and Wisconsin.

57. These were: Arkansas, Alabama, Missouri, New Jersey, Rhode Island, South Carolina, Vermont, Connecticut, Hawaii, Virginia, and West Virginia. However, West Virginia permitted fault to be considered only if the divorce had been obtained on fault grounds.

58. The states with equal-distribution rules are Arkansas, California, Florida, Idaho, and Louisiana.

59. They are Alabama, Georgia, Maryland, Mississippi, and West Virginia.

60. Uniform Marriage and Divorce Act, §307.

61. They were: Alaska, Colorado, Delaware, Illinois, Indiana, Iowa, Kentucky, Maine, Massachusetts, Minnesota, Missouri, Montana, Nebraska, New York, Ohio, Oregon, Pennsylvania, Rhode Island, Tennessee, Vermont, Virginia, and Wisconsin.

62. These were Colorado, Kentucky, Maine, Missouri, Ohio, and Pennsylvania.

63. Uniform Marriage and Divorce Act, §308.

64. Martha L. Fineman, "Implementing Equality: Ideology, Contradiction and Social Change—A Study of the Rhetoric and Results in the Regulation of the Consequences of Divorce," *Wisconsin Law Review* 1983 (November): 789–886.

65. This account is based on newspaper accounts, interviews with many of the legislative participants, and legislative documents.

66. For instance, she insisted on being called "chairman" rather than "chairwoman" or "chairperson." Transcript of hearings jointly sponsored by the Matrimonial Law Committee of the New York Lawyers' Association and the Association of the Bar of the City of New York, 13 January 1972, 27, 63, typescript.

67. Orr v. Orr, 440 US 268 (1979).

68. See the description of this group in Jo Freeman, *The Politics of Women's Liberation* (New York: David McKay, 1975), 71–102.

69. Paula Peters, "Property Disposition upon Divorce in Mary-

land: An Analysis of the New Statute," *Baltimore Law Review* 8 (1979): 383–86.

Chapter Eight

1. H. Jay Folberg and Marva Graham, "Joint Custody of Children Following Divorce," *University of California Davis Law Review* 12 (1979): 530–32.

2. People ex rel Nickerson, 19 Wend. 16 (N.Y. 1837), quoted by Jamil S. Zainaldin, "The Emergence of a Modern American Family Law: Child Custody, Adoption and the Courts 1796–1851," *Northwestern University Law Review* 73 (1979); 1064.

3. Mercein v. People ex rel Barry, 25 Wend. 65 (N.Y. 1840), quoted by Zainaldin, "Emergence," 1066.

4. On the development of custody law generally, see Zainaldin "Emergence"; Folberg and Graham, "Joint Custody," 523–40; Michael Grossberg, "Who Gets the Child? Custody, Guardianship and the Rise of a Judicial Patriarchy in Nineteenth-Century America," *Feminist Studies* 9 (Summer 1983): 235–60; and Deborah A. Luepnitz, *Child Custody* (Lexington, Mass.: Lexington Books, 1982).

5. Anne M. Boylan, "Growing Up Female in America 1800–1860," in Joseph M. Hawers and N. Ray Hiner, eds., *American Childhood: A Research Guide and Historical Handbook* (Westport, Conn.: Greenwood Press, 1985), 156.

6. Zainaldin, "Emergence," 1073.

7. Jenkins v. Jenkins, 173 Wis 592, 181 N.W. 826, 826 (1921) as quoted in Folberg and Graham, "Joint Custody," 532.

8. Zainaldin, "Emergence," 1074.

9. These developments are summarized by Priscilla Ferguson Clement, "The City and the Child, 1860–1885," in Hawes and Hiner, eds., *American Childhood: A Research Guide and Historical Handbook* (Westport, Conn.: Greenwood Press, 1985), 235–72, and by Ronald D. Cohen, "Child-Saving and Progressivism, 1885–1915," in Hawes and Hiner, *American Childhood*, 273–309.

10. Viviana A. Zelizer, *Pricing the Priceless Child: The Changing Social Value of Children* (New York: Basic Books, 1985).

11. Zelizer, *Pricing the Priceless Child.*

12. Not all these standards were in every code or appellate precedent. However, see Minn. Stat. Ann. §518.17 (1978).

13. Frank F. Furstenberg, Jr., Christine Winquist Nord, James L. Peterson, and Nicholas Zill, "The Life Course of Children of Divorce: Marital Disruption and Parental Contact," *American Sociological Review* 48 (October 1983); 656–68; Paul G. Glick, "Children of

Divorced Parents in Demographic Perspective," *Journal of Social Issues* 35 (1979); 170–82.

14. Furstenberg et al., "The Life Course of Children," 663.

15. Judith Cassetty, *Child Support and Public Policy* (Lexington, Mass.: Lexington Books, 1978), 1–21.

16. *Congressional Quarterly Almanac, 1984,* 463.

17. Uniform Marriage and Divorce Act, §402.

18. Robert J. Levy, "Uniform Marriage and Divorce Legislation: A Preliminary Analysis Prepared for the Special Committee on Divorce of the National Conference of Commissioners on Uniform State Laws," typescript, 1968, 224; henceforth referred to as Levy monograph.

19. Ibid., 225.

20. Ibid., 237.

21. Uniform Marriage and Divorce Act, §402. The official comment for the Uniform Marriage and Divorce Act reads: "The preference for the mother as custodian of young children when all things are equal, for example, is simply a shorthand method of expressing the best interest of children—and this section enjoins judges to decide custody cases according to that general standard." Editors of Family Law Reporter, *Desk Guide to the Uniform Marriage and Divorce Act* (Washington: Bureau of National Affairs, 1974), 43.

22. Uniform Marriage and Divorce Act, §409 (a) and (b).

23. Joseph Goldstein, Anna Freud, and Albert J. Solnit, *Beyond the Best Interests of the Child* (New York: Free Press, 1973), 6. In the 1979 edition of their book, the authors reinterpret their ban to extend only to *court-enforced* visitation on the grounds that court orders undermine the authority of the custodial parent. They retain, however, their hostility to split or joint custody. See pp. 116–33 of their 1979 edition.

24. Carol B. Stack, "Who Owns the Child? Divorce and Child Custody Decisions in Middle-Class Families," *Social Problems* 23 (1976): 505–15.

25. See Georgia Dullea, "Joint Custody: Is Sharing the Child a Dangerous Idea?" *New York Times,* 24 May 1976, 24; Molinoff, "After Divorce, Given them a Father Too," *Newsday,* 5 October 1975; Charlotte Baum, "The Best of Both Parents," *New York Times Magazine,* 31 October 1976, 44–48; Mary Alice Kellog, "Joint Custody," *Newsweek,* 24 January 1977, 56; and "One Child, Two Homes," *Time Magazine,* 29 January 1979, 61.

26. Joan Schulman, "Who's Looking After the Children?" *Family Advocate* 5 (Fall 1982): 31–37.

27. 5 May 1975, 18.

28. 30 October 1975, 33.

29. 24 May 1975, 24; Magazine, 31 October 1976, 24; 6 March 1977, 22.

30. 24 January 1977, 56.

31. Mel Roman and William Haddad, *The Disposable Parent: The Case for Joint Custody* (New York: Holt, Rinehart, and Winston, 1978), 8–9.

32. A LEXIS search for citations to both books between 1974 and 1979 in New York, California, Illinois, and Michigan found eighteen references to Goldstein et al., but none to Roman and Haddad.

33. Kristin Luker, *Abortion and the Politics of Motherhood* (Berkeley: University of California Press, 1984).

34. James Cook, interview with author, Los Angeles, 5 June 1987.

35. California Assembly Interim Committee on the Judiciary, Transcript of Proceedings on Domestic Relations Law, 8–9 January 1964, testimony by Peter Hoffman representing United States Divorce Reform, Inc., 207.

36. California Assembly Interim Committee, 210.

37. *Minneapolis Star,* 14 January 1969, on U.S. Divorce Reform League's campaign to reform alimony and child custody. Levy regarded such groups as nothing more than "fringe groups." Levy monograph, 2, note 6; 102, note 511.

38. For California, personal letter to the author from Deborah M. DeBow, Counsel of California Assembly Committee on Judiciary, 10 February 1986, and Nancy K. Lemon, "Joint Custody as a Statutory Presumption: California's New Civil Code Sections 4600 and 4600.5," *Golden Gate University Law Review* 11 (1981): 505. For Louisiana, typescript of House Civil Law and Procedure Committee Hearing on 7 June 1982 on HB 1194.

39. *New York Times,* 2 January 1973, 39.

40. *New York Times,* 29 July 1973, 61.

41. The author sent a mail questionnaire to legislative leaders in the twenty-six states which had adopted joint custody legislation in recent years. The following paragraphs are based in part on the responses which were obtained.

42. The states identified in the survey were Alaska, California, Connecticut, Florida, Indiana, Louisiana, Maine, Michigan, Missouri, Montana, New Hampshire, Nevada, Ohio, and Pennsylvania.

43. The following is based on an interview with James Cook, 5 June 1987.

44. Jo Freeman, *The Politics of Women's Liberation* (New York: David McKay, 1975), 103–46.

45. Lemon, "Joint Custody," 505.

46. In the same survey, feminist organizations were mentioned in only five states: California, Connecticut, Indiana, Missouri, and New Hampshire.

47. Katharine T. Bartlett and Carol B. Stack, "Joint Custody, Feminism and the Dependency Dilemma," *Berkeley Women's Law Journal* (Winter 1986): 503–5.

48. Joanne Schulman and Valerie Pitt, "Second Thoughts on Joint Child Custody: Analysis of Legislation and Its Implications for Women and Children," *Golden Gate University Law Review* 12 (1982): 538–77; Fran Olsen, "The Politics of Family Law," *Law and Inequality* 2 (1984): 12–19; Bartlett and Stack, "Joint Custody", 505–7.

49. This account is based on Lemon, "Joint Custody," and on the responses to a questionnaire sent to legislative leaders in California.

50. SB 477.

51. AB 1480 as quoted in Lemon, "Joint Custody," 505.

52. This amendment originated with a cultural anthropologist, Diane Trombetta, according to Lemon, "Joint Custody," 513.

53. Ibid.

54. There is a note from a leader of the fathers' groups, James Cook, attached to her testimony to the Senate Committee with the following message: "Please support this fine woman in her unselfish willingness to strive for equality between parents . . . This is an unsolicited remark by James Cook; and I urge you to direct counseling cases to Diane Trombetta."

55. E.g., Bridgette Brodenheimer, a faculty member of the University of California Davis Law School and a well-known expert in child custody law; also Anne L. Diamond, a colleague of Bodenheimer's. Letters in possession of author.

56. Statement of 4 June 1979, in possession of author.

57. Representative Donelon at Hearing of House Civil Law and Procedure Committee, 7 June 1982, typescript.

58. Masha M. Mason, Staff Attorney, Louisiana Senate, letter to author, 27 December 1985.

59. Louisiana Civil Code, Chap. 3, Art. 146.

60. Questionnaires from Rep. Bruce M. Bolin and from Dr. L. R. Savoie, January 1986.

61. Official Transcript, Illinois Senate, 10, 22, 25 June 1982; Official Transcript, Illinois General Assembly, 10, 20 May, 27–28 June 1982.

62. Official Transcript, Illinois Senate Debates, 23 May 1985, 222. Ellipses in original.

Chapter Nine

1. Howard S. Erlanger, Elizabeth Chambliss, and Marygold S. Melli, "Cooperation or Coercion? Informal Settlement in the Divorce Context," University of Wisconsin-Madison Law School, Disputes Processing Research Program, Working Papers, Series 7, March 1986.

2. Austin Sarat and William L. F. Felstiner, "Law and Strategy in the Divorce Lawyer's Office," *Law and Society Review* 20 (1986): 79–92; Austin Sarat and William L. F. Felstiner, "The Ideology of Divorce: Law in the Lawyer's Office," paper prepared for workshop on the Study of the Interaction between Lawyer and Client, Rijksuniversiteit, Groningen, The Netherlands, October 1984.

3. On the state of historical statistics regarding details of divorce proceedings, see Dan Hopson, Jr., "The Economics of a Divorce: A Pilot Empirical Study at the Trial Court Level," *Kansas Law Review* 11 (1962): 107–55.

4. W. P. C. Phear, J. C. Beck, B. B. Hauser, S. C. Clark, and R. A. Whitney, "An Empirical Study of Custody Agreements: Joint Versus Sole Legal Custody," in Jay Folberg, ed., *Joint Custody and Shared Parenting,* (Washington: Bureau of National Affairs and Association of Family and Conciliation Courts, 1984), 143, write: "Despite the legal distinctions between fault and no-fault pleas, it is recognized that couples sometimes agree to divorce under one of the 'fault' categories in order to minimize the wait between filing for a divorce and the divorce becoming final." An observer in Utah has noted that most divorces in that state are still obtained under the fault ground of mental cruelty despite the availability of no-fault divorce. Stephen J. Bahr, letter to author, 6 February 1987.

5. An example is California's Donald Grunsky, a senator for more than thirty years who took more pride in his sponsorship of the state's new penal code and new education code than in his sponsorship of the no-fault divorce law, although his contribution to no-fault was an essential one. Personal interview, Watsonville, Ca., 13 February 1985.

6. Stephen L. Sass, "The Iowa No-Fault Dissolution of Marriage Law in Action," *South Dakota Law Review* 18 (1973): 636–37, 649.

7. Alan H. Frank, John J. Berman, and Stanley F. Mazur-Hart, "No Fault Divorce and the Divorce Rate: The Nebraska Experience—An Interrupted Time Series Analysis and Commentary," *Nebraska Law Review* 58 (1978): 17–25.

8. Ibid.

9. Elayne Carol Berg, "Irreconcilable Differences: California

Courts Respond to No-Fault Dissolutions," *Loyola of Los Angeles Law Review* 7 (1974); Leonard E. Bellinson, "Changing Dynamics in Attorney-Client Relationship Due to No-Fault Divorce Legislation," *Case & Comment* 79 (March–April 1974): 30–31.

10. Sass, "Iowa No-Fault," 637.

11. See, for instance, Berg, "Irreconcilable Differences," 453–88.

12. Mary Ann Glendon, "Family Law Reform in the 1980's," *Louisiana Law Review* 44 (1984): 1556.

13. Harriet N. Cohen and Adrian S. Hillman, "New York Courts Have Not Recognized Women as Equal Marriage Partners," *Equitable Distribution Reporter* 5 (March 1985): 95. On the other hand, contrary conclusions were drawn from a group of mediated (rather than adjudicated) cases by John W. Heister, "Property Allocation in Mediation: An Examination of Distribution Relative to Equality and to Gender," *Mediation Quarterly* 17 (Fall 1987): 97–98.

14. Martha L. Fineman, "Implementing Equality: Ideology, Contradiction and Social Change—A Study of the Rhetoric and Results in the Regulation of the Consequences of Divorce," *Wisconsin Law Review* 1983 (November): 885.

15. Adele H. Hendrickson and Joanne Schulman, "Trends in Child Custody Law: What They Mean for Women" (National Center on Women and Family Law, New York, 1981, mimeographed).

16. Nancy D. Polikoff, "Gender and Child-Custody Determinations: Exploding Myths," in Irene Diamond, ed., *Families, Politics, and Public Policy: A Feminist Dialogue on Women and the State* (New York: Longman, 1983), 187, 197.

17. Thomas J. Espenshade, "The Economic Consequences of Divorce," *Journal of Marriage and the Family* 41 (1979): 615–25; Frank L. Mott and Sylvia F. Moore, "The Causes and Consequences of Marital Breakdown," in Frank L. Mott, ed., *Women, Work, and Family: Dimensions of Change in American Society* (Lexington, Mass.: Lexington Books, 1978), 113–35; Gilbert Nestel, Jacqueline Mercier, and Lois B. Shaw, "Economic Consequences of Midlife Change in Marital Status," in Lois B. Shaw, ed., *Unplanned Careers: The Working Lives of Middle-Aged Women* (Lexington, Mass.: Lexington Books, 1983), 109–25; Greg J. Duncan and Saul D. Hoffman, "A Reconsideration of the Economic Consequences of Marital Dissolution," *Demography* 22 (November 1985): 485–97.

18. Lenore Weitzman, *The Divorce Revolution* (New York: Free Press, 1985). The book was the co-winner of a prize in 1986 from the American Sociological Association as the best work on a social problem and was widely reviewed in the popular media.

19. The samples and research techniques are described in Weitzman, *Divorce Revolution*, 403–15.

20. Ibid., 382–83.

21. Lenore J. Weitzman and Ruth B. Dixon, "The Transformation of Marriage Through No-Fault Divorce: The Case of the United States," in John M. Eekelaar and Sanford N. Katz, eds., *Marriage and Cohabitation in Contemporary Society* (Toronto: Butterworth, 1980), 143–53.

22. Weitzman, *Divorce Revolution*, 366.

23. Ibid., 78.

24. Lenore J. Weitzman, "The Economics of Divorce: Social and Economic Consequences of Property, Alimony and Child Support Awards," *UCLA Law Review* 28 (August 1981): 1181–1268, and Weitzman, *Divorce Revolution*, 70–142.

25. Weitzman, *Divorce Revolution*, 143–214.

26. Ibid., 310–18.

27. Weitzman, "Economics of Divorce," 1251, and Weitzman, *Divorce Revolution*, 338.

28. Elizabeth H. Peters, "Marriage and Divorce: Informational Constraints and Private Contracting," *American Economic Review* 76 (June 1986): 437–54.

29. I develop this theme more fully in Herbert Jacob, "Faulting No-Fault," *American Bar Foundation Research Journal* 1986 (Fall): 773–81; see also in this same journal issue Marygold S. Melli, "Constructing a Social Problem: The Post-Divorce Plight of Women and Children," 759–72, and Weitzman's reply in Lenore Weitzman, "Bringing the Law Back In," 791–97.

30. Robert Schoen, Harry N. Greenblatt, and Robert B. Mielke, "California's Experience with Non-Adversary Divorce," *Demography* 12 (May 1975): 223–43; Gerald C. Wright, Jr. and Dorothy M. Stetson, "The Impact of No-Fault Divorce Law Reform on Divorce in American States," *Journal of Marriage and the Family* 40 (August 1978): 575–80; Frank et al., "No Fault Divorce and the Divorce Rate," 1–99; Harvey J. Sepler, "Measuring the Effects of No-Fault Divorce Laws Across the Fifty States: Quantifying a Zeitgeist," *Family Law Quarterly* 15 (Spring 1981): 65–102.

31. Schoen, Greenblatt, and Mielke, "California's Experience."

32. Jessica Pearson and Nancy Thoennes, "Will This Divorced Woman Receive Child Support?" *Judges Journal* (Winter 1986): 40–46.

33. Howard H. Irving, Michael Benjamin, and Nicolas Trocme, "Shared Parenting: An Empirical Analysis Utilizing a Large Canadian

Data Base," in Jay Folberg, ed., *Joint Custody and Shared Parenting,* (Washington: Bureau of National Affairs and Association of Family and Conciliation Courts, 1984), 132–33; see also Pearson and Thoennes, "Will This Divorced Woman Receive Child Support?"

34. Frederic W. Jr. Ilfeld, Holly Zingale Ilfeld, and John R. Alexander, "Does Joint Custody Work? A First Look at Outcome Data of Relitigation," in Folberg, *Joint Custody,* 136–41. A study of Massachusetts custody relitigation appears to show joint custody cases returning to court more frequently than sole custody; however, those joint custody cases do not involve joint physical custody arrangements and are in many ways indistinguishable from sole custody in other states. W. P. C. Phear, J. C. Beck, B. B. Hauser, S. C. Clark, and R. A. Whitney, "An Empirical Study of Custody Agreements: Joint Versus Sole Legal Custody," in Folberg, *Joint Custody,* 142–58.

35. Martha Minow, "Consider the Consequences," *Michigan Law Review* 84 (February–April 1986): 914.

36. Herma Hill Kay, "An Appraisal of California's No-Fault Divorce Law," *California Law Review* 75 (1987): 310–19.

Chapter Ten

1. John W. Kingdon, *Congressmen's Voting Decisions* (New York: Harper & Row, 1973), 230.

2. Barbara J. Nelson, *Making an Issue of Child Abuse: Political Agenda Setting for Social Problems* (Chicago: University of Chicago Press, 1984).

3. John P. Heinz, Robert W. Gettleman, and Morris A. Seeskin, "Legislative Politics and the Criminal Law," *Northwestern University Law Review* 64 (July–August 1969): 277–358; Richard A. Berk, Harold Brackman, and Selma Lesser, *A Measure of Justice: An Empirical Study of Changes in the California Penal Code 1955–1971* (New York: Academic Press, 1977).

4. Heinz et al., "Legislative Politics," 349.

5. Berk et al., *Measure of Justice,* 298.

6. Kenneth Mladenka, "The Urban Bureaucracy and the Chicago Political Machine: Who Gets What and the Limits to Political Control," *American Political Science Review* 74 (December 1980); 991–98; Robert L. Lineberry, *Equality and Urban Policy* (Beverly Hills: Sage, 1977); Frank S. Levy, Arnold J. Meltsner, and Aaron Wildavsky, *Urban Outcomes* (Berkeley: University of California Press, 1974).

7. Anne L. Spitzer, "Moving and Storage of Postdivorce Children: Relocation, the Constitution, and the Courts," *Arizona State Law*

Journal 1985 (1985): 1–78; Sheehan, "Post-Divorce Child Custody and Family Relocation," *Harvard Women's Law Journal* 9 (1986): 135–52.

8. Judith S. Wallerstein and Shauna B. Corbin, "Father-Child Relationships After Divorce: Child Support and Educational Opportunity," *Family Law Quarterly* 20 (1986): 109–28.

Index

abortion, 25
adultery, as ground for divorce, 1,
4, 30, 34; and alimony, 1; and
child custody, 1
adversarial divorce, 68
alimony, 3, 112–16, 122; in California, 56, 59, 60. *See also*
maintenance
American Bar Association, Family
Law Section, 35, 67, 73, 119–20
Archbishop of Canterbury, 45–46
Arkansas, and no-fault divorce, 81
Auerbach, Marshall, 97

bar associations, and the spread of
no-fault divorce, 85–86
Bar Association of the City of New
York, and divorce law reform,
39, 40
Basch, Norma, 107
best interests of child, 56, 130–31
Bianchi, Suzanne M., 19
Blake, Nelson, 33
Brown, Edmund Sr., 53, 54

California, and adoption of no-
fault, 43–61, 90; evaluation of
divorce reform in, 159–64; influence upon NCCUSL, 71; joint
custody legislation in, 139–41;
property provisions, 121–23
Catholic church, and divorce, 30,

56–57; and marital property reform, 123; and NCCUSL, 71–72;
and opposition to divorce, 35–
37, 86–97, 97, 98
Cheadle, Elizabeth A., 115
child support, 2, 8, 56, 127–44,
132. *See also* joint custody
Cobb, Robert, 13
Cobb, Jennie-Keith, 13
community property, 113
conciliation, 31, 41, 42

Degler, Carl, 116
diffusion networks: and marital
property reform, 121–25; and
spread of no-fault divorce, 88–89
Dinkelspiel, Richard, 51, 57
Divorce Reform League, 32
Dwight, Timothy, 31

evaluation: criteria for, 148–50; of
joint custody by lawyers, 157–
59; of marital property reforms
by lawyers, 157–58; of no-fault
divorce by lawyers, 154–56

family court, 54, 61
fathers' groups, and joint custody,
137–38, 140, 142
feminist movement, 21–24; and divorce law reform, 168, 172; and
evaluation of divorce law re-